Reading Matters 2

SECOND EDITION

Reading Matters ❷

An Interactive Approach to Reading

Mary Lee Wholey

Continuing Education Language Institute
Concordia University

▷ For teaching notes, answer key, and other related instructor material, as well as for additional student activities related to this book, go to *college.hmco.com/pic/wholeytwo2e.*

▷ To obtain access to the Houghton Mifflin ESL instructor sites, call 1-800-733-1717.

Houghton Mifflin Company

Boston　New York

Publisher: Patricia A. Coryell
Editor in Chief: Suzanne Phelps Weir
Sponsoring Editor: Joann Kozyrev
Senior Development Editor: Kathleen Sands Boehmer
Development Editor: Sharla Zwirek
Editorial Assistant: Evangeline Bermas
Senior Project Editor: Margaret Park Bridges
Associate Manufacturing Buyer: Brian Pieragostini
Executive Marketing Manager: Annamarie Rice
Marketing Associate: Andrew Whitacre

Cover Images: Background photograph: © Photodisc Photography/Veer.com.
Thumbnail photographs from left to right: Noted author Jeanne Wakatsuki Houston reads from one of her works at the Cesar Chavez Public Library in Salinas, CA (AP Photo/The Salinas Californian, Richard Green); 1919 photo of Albert Einstein in his study, age 40 (AP Photo/NY Times); Dalai Lama reads through his speech during a function at Dharamsala, India (AP Photo/Angus McDonald); Young Helen Keller reading a book in Braille © Bettman/CORBIS; Members of the Philadelphia Eagles relax in the stands at Alltel Stadium in Jacksonville, Fla. (AP Photo/Stephan Savoia)

Text and Graph Credits: Copyrights and acknowledgments appear on page 249, which constitutes an extension of the copyright page.

Photo Credits: p. 0: © Bob Torrez; p. 15: © Jim Mayfield; p. 19: © Parrot Pascal/CORBIS SYGMA; p. 30: © H. Winkler/A. B./zefa/CORBIS; p. 42: © Michael Newman/PhotoEdit; p. 55: © Scott T. Baxter/Getty Images; p. 58: © Michael A. Keller/zefa/CORBIS; p. 68: © Ken Huang/Getty Images; p. 76: © Michael Newman/PhotoEdit; p. 82: © C Squared Studios/Getty Images; p. 91: © James Shaffer/PhotoEdit; p. 95: © Cindy Charles/PhotoEdit; p. 108: © Gavin Kingcome Photography/Getty Images; p. 114: © Fred Felleman/Getty Images; p. 116: Images provided courtesy of the International Dark-Sky Association (http://www.darksky.org); p. 131: © John Giustina/Getty Images; p. 135: © Art Wolfe/Getty Images; p. 162: © Tim Crosby; p. 167: © Shonna Valeska 2005; p. 206: © Jonathan Blair/CORBIS; p. 212: © CORBIS; p. 220: © Underwood & Underwood/CORBIS; p. 225: © Ralph White/CORBIS

Printed in the U.S.A.

Library of Congress Control Number: 2005934054

Student Text
   ISBN-10: 0-618-47513-3
   ISBN-13: 978-0-618-47513-1

Instructor's Examination Copy
   ISBN-10: 0-618-73257-8
   ISBN-13: 978-0-618-73257-9

23456789-CRS-10 09 08 07 06

Contents

Introduction to the Second Edition

The *Reading Matters* series is a four-level reading program comprising texts at the high-beginning/low-intermediate, intermediate, high-intermediate, and advanced levels. It fosters the development of active readers through a multifaceted approach to interaction: interaction with the text, with other readers, and with readings from sources beyond the classroom. This new edition includes new and updated readings as well as additional readings in the "Expanding Your Language" section of each chapter. The *Reading Matters* series features stimulating extensive reading combined with intensive practice provided by well designed tasks that develop both fluency and accuracy at each level. The series incorporates the latest approaches to teaching productive strategies—from understanding the purpose and nature of different texts to guessing meaning from context, learning vocabulary for academic and professional success, and learning how to access information in the media and over the Internet.

In brief the series provides for:

▶ The development of active readers through interaction with a variety of texts, with other readers through reading-retell tasks, and with authentic reading outside of the classroom.

▶ Thematic units featuring high-interest, level-appropriate, informative topics that include texts about culture, science, the environment, business, innovation, sports, and entertainment.

▶ A wide variety of reading types, such as articles, interviews, essays, charts, and graphs.

▶ A skills and strategies overview of the comprehensive reading skills and strategies in each chapter that feature the development of critical thinking and information processing.

▶ Opportunities for personal reading, writing, and speaking activities.

▶ An index of key vocabulary aimed at both academic and professional needs (provided at *college.hmco.com/pic/wholeytwo2e*).

▶ Access to the *Reading Matters* Online Study Center website, which includes individualized learning and testing materials, at *college.hmco.com/pic/wholeytwo2e*.

Extensive Reading

To develop fluency in reading, students need significant exposure to text—that is, extensive reading. Extensive reading provides the opportunity to develop automatic text-processing skills. *Reading Matters* offers high-interest reading selections of sufficient length so that readers get the chance to increase the amount of time spent in silent reading. Variety in text styles is an important component of extensive reading. The series features a variety of styles and genres including articles, interviews, graphs, and charts, so that readers develop an awareness of the scope of reading as well as the various purposes for which texts are written. Authentic texts or adapted authentic texts are used at appropriate levels.

Intensive Reading

Reading Matters features thematically-related units on topics of interest and relevancy today. These topics range from social issues, scientific advances, the environment, and the business world to the fields of leisure, entertainment, and culture. The activities in each unit help students develop fluency and accuracy in reading by activating two complementary text processing methods: top-down and bottom-up.

The Process of Reading

Top-Down

Reading Matters enhances the approaches readers use to understand reading globally. In this series, the readers' background knowledge of the topic and critical thinking skills are engaged and readers are encouraged to make predictions about what they expect to find in a text. The reader reads to confirm or modify these predictions and begins to build a mental framework of the information in the reading selection. Awareness of rhetorical patterns, such as chronological ordering, cause and effect relationships, and other discourse features aids in the comprehension of information from the reading. In addition, *Reading Matters* helps the reader develop an awareness of the range of reading strategies, such as skimming, scanning, or previewing, that readers have at their disposal. The ability to apply these strategies appropriately is an important component of reading competency.

Bottom-Up

Knowledge of grammar and vocabulary has an effect on reading ability. Although readers can predict content from their knowledge of text structure or their background knowledge, a certain level of vocabulary recognition is required for processing text. *Reading Matters* introduces and develops vocabulary-building skills through such activities as guessing from context, recognizing meaning, grouping words, and identifying the use of special terms. Well-designed tasks help the reader learn new vocabulary and key words in the text. In the context of thematic units, the reader's vocabulary develops naturally through exposure to a range of texts. Students engage in a gradual process of acquiring key vocabulary by building from a basic level of vocabulary to a wider net of related terms. Students build their understanding through repeated use of language that contains key concepts and information.

In addition to a solid vocabulary, fluent readers have a good knowledge of syntactic structure.

Actively examining the important grammatical features of a text provides a meaningful context for this kind of learning. To build reading competency, the amount of exposure to reading as well as the identification and practice of learning strategies for both vocabulary and grammar are tremendously important. *Reading Matters* provides direction to readers through activities in the "Vocabulary Building," "Expanding Your Language," and "Read On" sections.

Skills Integration and Interaction

Reading is an active process. Interaction between and among students helps to facilitate this process. In exchanging ideas about the information in a text, readers confirm what they have understood. This confirmation process helps to develop accuracy in reading. It also provides a motivation as well as a clear purpose for reading. Interaction with other students can be best accomplished when speaking tasks are an integral part of a reading activity or the activity leads to the undertaking of writing tasks.

The interrelationship of skills integration and interaction requires a holistic approach to task design. The activities in *Reading Matters* are sequenced, and the recycling of tasks in various combinations allows the progressive development of reading competency in ways that are fresh and effective. The tasks are structured so that the learner builds skills and strategies progressively but in ways that offers challenge as well as variety. In *Reading Matters*, the reader uses and reuses the language of the selection both implicitly—to bolster an answer—and explicitly, as in the exchange of information from paired reading selections that provide complementary or contrasting information on a topic. Readers orally explain the information from their reading selection to readers who chose a different selection. Then, together, they apply that information to carry out a new activity.

Text Organization

Reading Matters 2 contains six thematic units with three chapters in each unit. In the second edition, each chapter features two to four reading selections. Many readings have been updated and new readings have been introduced. The unit themes feature topics of high interest to both academically-oriented and general audiences. Most importantly, the selections are of sufficient length for students to progressively develop fluency in reading. Through the chapter readings, students are able to build a rich semantic network without sacrificing variety so that interest in the topic is not exhausted. Within each unit, reading selections are structured so that the information from one selection can be compared with another.

You can choose among the chapters of a unit selectively to suit the needs of various program types and teaching approaches. Complexity in both text type and length, and difficulty in task type are structured to build gradually from chapter to chapter and unit to unit. Some overlap in level of language and task is built into each of the texts in the *Reading Matters* series so that you can accommodate the various levels of students within a class.

Unit Organization

Each unit in *Reading Matters 2* features the following components:

▶ Introducing the Topic: This introductory section identifies the theme. It features the unit opener photo and quote, which are designed to stimulate the readers' curiosity about and prior experience with the theme, or its personal relevance. The tasks are interactive and draw on a variety of media: text, photos, and graphics.

▶ Chapters: The three chapters in each unit present various topics loosely related to the theme.

Chapter Organization

For each of the reading selections the following tasks are presented:

▶ **Chapter Openers** include pre-reading reflection and discussion questions, graphs, questionnaires, surveys, or illustrations. The purpose of this section is to stimulate discussion of key ideas and concepts presented in the reading and to introduce key vocabulary. Encourage students to explain their ideas as completely as possible. Teach students strategies for maximizing their interaction, such as turn taking, eliciting responses from all group members, and naming a group leader and reporter. Whenever possible, re-form groups to give students a chance to talk more until they feel comfortable with the topic. Elicit key ideas and language from the students.

▶ **Exploring and Understanding Reading** contains content questions of varying levels of complexity. These questions guide students in the development of their reading strategies for improving general comprehension, developing an awareness of text structure, and evaluating the content of a text in detail. Emphasize the purpose of the activity and how it is tied to the development of a particular strategy. Point out the ways in which students can apply their skills to reading assignments. Help students build their tolerance for uncertainty. Point out that the purpose of comparing and checking their answers with the information in the reading is to verify as well as to become familiar with the information in the reading. Act as a resource to help students find the accurate information. An answer key that the instructor can use as needed is provided on the *Reading Matters* website at *college.hmco.com/pic/wholeytwo2e*.

▶ **Paired Readings** include interactive Recapping, Retelling, Reacting to the Reading, and Discussing the Story activities that involve oral presentation of information from the readings, oral exchanges of information, and discussion that involves critical evaluation of ideas, including comparison/contrast and debate. At this level, talking about the reading they do is crucial for improving students' language use. Emphasize the importance of explaining the information in as natural and conversational a style as possible. Help students to develop their skill at extracting important information from a text by pointing out the purpose of note taking, highlighting, and underlining key information. Emphasize the importance of practicing at home for in-class presentations.

▶ **Vocabulary Building** comprises tasks that introduce vocabulary-building strategies such as the understanding of key terms, the interrelationship of grammatical structure and meaning, using context cues, and developing other aids to the fluent processing of reading selections. This edition adds exercises in each chapter that focus on learning the meaning of verbs and working with word form and function to foster the understanding of academic and general vocabulary.

▶ **Expanding Your Language** presents activities that offer students additional opportunities to use the material and strategies in the chapter. This section often includes additional extended readings. Encourage students to use these activities to further their own comprehension of the readings. Through these activities, students can improve their speaking and writing fluency.

▶ **Read On: Taking It Further** presents opportunities for personal reading and related activities, including suggestions for further reading as well as reading and writing journal entries, keeping a vocabulary log, and word play. Although most of this work will be done outside of class, time can be found in the class schedule to report on some of the activities. This gives students a purpose for the work and practice in developing their reading skills and strategies.

Reading Matters Online Study Center Website

Students gain confidence in their reading abilities as they discover how to access information more easily from the press, over the Internet, and in their professions or fields of study. The Internet activities give students a chance to consolidate and extend their reading skills. Using the *Reading Matters* website offers students the opportunity for productive work on an individual basis at any time of day or night that's convenient for them. Students are directed to the Online Study Center website at the end of each chapter.

Reading Matters Online Teaching Center Website

As with all Houghton Mifflin textbooks, there is a specific website devoted to necessary teaching tools that come in handy while using the text. Instructors using *Reading Matters* can access useful chapter notes and the answer key at the site. In addition, there are downloadable chapter tests that instructors can administer to students. These tests focus on comprehension skills and important vocabulary. Finally, a sample syllabus is included for instructors who need some guidelines about how to use the text effectively throughout the semester. To access the Online Teaching Center, go to *college.hmco.com/pic/wholeytwo2e.*

Acknowledgments

I am grateful to Susan Maguire, who first suggested the idea for the series. A special thanks goes to Kathy Sands Boehmer and Sharla Zwirek, who have been an invaluable help throughout the lengthy process of bringing this manuscript into its present form. Thanks also to Margaret Bridges and the rest of the production and editorial staff at Houghton Mifflin.

My gratitude to the people who read the manuscript and offered useful suggestions and critical comments: Marcella Farina, *University of Central Florida;* Patrick Kennedy, *University of Toledo;* Richard Skinner, *Hudson County Community College;* Sandra Sklarew, *George Mason University;* and Julie Thornton, *University of Iowa.*

I would like to acknowledge the support and inspiring work of colleagues and students at the Continuing Education Language Institute (CELI) of Concordia University in Montreal. A special thanks goes to Adrianne Sklar for her advice and suggestions after reading drafts of the material. The continuing support of Lili Ullmann, Phyllis Vogel, and Nadia Henein has been invaluable to me. Thank you also to Ioana Nicolae, who helped in the preparation of the answer key and the student online study activities.

Finally, thanks to my family—Jerry, Jonah, and Yael—who haven't given up on me, even though they've heard, "Can't right now, got to finish this work," for years on end.

Mary Lee Wholey

Reading Matters 2: Overview

Unit	Skills	Activities	Vocabulary	Expansion
UNIT 1 **Habits of a Lifetime**	• previewing (1) • using notes to explain ideas (1, 2, 3) • predicting (1, 2, 3) • note taking (1) • getting the main idea (3) • scanning (3) • using facts to make a case (3)	• categorizing (1) • evaluating information (1) • problem solving (1) • recapping and reacting (2) • giving an opinion (2) • comparing stories (2) • getting information from a graph (3) • answering a survey (3) • answering a questionnaire (3)	• using context to guess meaning (1) • meaning of verbs (1, 2, 3) • word form (1, 2, 3) • past tense verbs (1, 3) • sentence form (1) • synonyms (2, 3) • antonyms (2) • word play (3)	• topic writing (1, 3) • studying online (1, 2, 3) • taking a position (2) • two-minute taped talk (2, 3) • tell and retell (3) • topic reading (3) • reading journal (3) • keeping a vocabulary log (3) • organizing a personal dictionary (3)
UNIT 2 **Exploring Our Roots**	• previewing (4, 6) • getting the main idea (4) • scanning (4, 6) • note taking (5) • personalizing (6) • relating main ideas and details (6) • skimming (6)	• giving opinions (4, 6) • categorizing (5) • recapping, reacting to, and retelling a story (5) • comparing stories (5) • applying the information: finding reasons (6)	• meaning of verbs (4, 5, 6) • word form (4, 5, 6) • vocabulary in context: adjectives (4) • synonyms (4) • past tense verbs (5) • verb and preposition combinations (5, 6) • using context to guess meaning (6) • roots (6)	• oral presentation (4) • topic writing (4, 6) • opinion writing (4) • studying online (4, 5, 6) • role play (5) • reacting to a story (5) • tell and retell (6) • topic readings (6) • keeping a vocabulary log (6) • reading journal (6)
UNIT 3 **Money Matters**	• predicting (7, 9) • skimming (7, 8, 9) • getting information from a graph (8) • scanning (8) • recognizing sub-points (9) • developing ideas (9)	• problem solving (7) • evaluating information (7) • survey (8) • recapping, reacting to, and retelling a story (8) • giving an opinion (9) • answering *wh-* questions (9)	• expressions (7, 9) • meaning of verbs (7, 8, 9) • word form (7, 8, 9) • understanding definitions (7, 8) • matching meanings (8, 9) • synonyms (8) • phrasal verbs (9) • vocabulary in context: verbs (9) • word play (9)	• answering a questionnaire (7) • oral presentation (7) • topic writing (7, 9) • studying online (7, 8, 9) • reaction writing (8, 9) • survey (8) • debate (9) • topic reading (7, 8, 9) • reading journal (9) • keeping a vocabulary log (9)

Unit	Skills	Activities	Vocabulary	Expansion
UNIT 4 **Protecting Nature**	• personalizing (10) • skimming (10, 11, 12) • understanding explanations (10) • note taking: solutions (10), advantages (12) • highlighting (11) • using facts to argue (11) • previewing graphic information (12) • scanning (12) • understanding an extended example (12)	• highlighting to explain ideas (10) • recapping, reacting to, and retelling the story (11) • giving opinions (12) • thinking about problems and solutions (10, 12) • answering *wh*-questions (11, 12)	• meaning of verbs (10, 11, 12) • word form (10, 11, 12) • antonyms (10) • jigsaw sentences (10) • understanding definitions (11) • noun endings (11, 12) • past tense verbs (11) • synonyms (12) • prefix *re-* (12) • guessing meaning from context (12) • word play (12)	• reacting to the story (10) • writing about advantages (10) • reaction writing (10, 11, 12) • studying online (10, 11, 12) • two-minute taped talk (11) • summarizing and reacting (11) • topic writing (11, 12) • oral presentation (12) • topic reading (12) • reading newspaper articles (12)
UNIT 5 **Personality**	• predicting (13, 15) • previewing (13, 14) • chronology: following a story (13) • understanding descriptive details (13) • recognizing sub-points and details (14) • scanning for details (15)	• reacting to the story (13, 14, 15) • evaluating similarities and differences (13) • answering questions from notes (14) • making a chart to show results (14) • getting information from diagrams (15) • applying information: evaluating evidence (15)	• expressions (13) • meaning of verbs (13, 14, 15) • word form (13, 14, 15) • understanding definitions (13) • jigsaw sentences (13, 15) • suffixes (14, 15) • synonyms (14) • prefixes for antonyms (14, 15) • word play (15)	• retelling (13) • two-minute taped talk (13, 14) • topic writing (13, 14, 15) • personal writing (13) • studying online (13, 14, 15) • oral presentation (15) • free writing (15) • topic reading (13, 14) • reading newspaper articles (15)
UNIT 6 **The Search For Answers**	• predicting (16, 18) • skimming (16, 17, 18) • chronology: following a story (16) • understanding descriptive details (16) • scanning: for descriptive details (17), for facts (18) • finding the main ideas (18) • using highlighting to make a list (18)	• question making (16) • debating (16, 18) • note taking: chronology (17), descriptive details (18) • making a time line (17) • giving your opinion (17, 18) • using illustrations to understand ideas (18) • theorizing (18)	• meaning of verbs (16, 17, 18) • word form (16, 17, 18) • suffixes (16) • vocabulary in context: verbs (16, 17) • jigsaw sentences (16, 18) • synonyms (17) • descriptive language (17) • expressing possibility (18)	• two-minute taped talk (16, 17) • topic writing (16, 17) • studying online (16, 17, 18) • reaction writing (17) • role play/ interviewing (18) • writing a description (18) • topic reading (16, 17, 18) • reading journal (18) • keeping a vocabulary log (18)

UNIT 1

Habits of a Lifetime

To be prepared is
half the victory.

—*Miguel Cervantes*

Introducing the Topic

The daily events of our lives have a great effect on our feelings of happiness, success, and satisfaction. In this unit you will read about some of the habits that shape our lives. Chapter 1 is about how to develop habits that help students be successful. Chapter 2 is about the lifestyles of two people who have led long and interesting lives. In Chapter 3 there are some interesting facts about sleeping habits and their effects on us.

Points of Interest

Discussion Questions

Habits Think about these questions. Share your ideas with a partner or in a small group.

1. What are some common habits people have?

   Examples: Getting up early in the morning
   Exercising in the evening
   Eating dinner at 6:00

2. How do our habits affect our lives both positively and negatively?
3. Why do you think people try to change their habits?

Understanding Expressions

Here are some sayings about habits. Write what you think each one means. Discuss your ideas with a partner or in a small group. Try to agree on a meaning.

1. Good habits are so much easier to give up than bad ones.
2. Old habits die hard.
3. Make success a habit.

1 Where Does the Time Go?

▶Chapter Openers

Categorizing

> **Reading Tip**

Thinking about a topic before reading helps you understand the ideas more easily. ■

▷ What do you do to succeed in school? Check (✔) whether you think each of these activities is a good or poor study skill.

Activities	Study Skills	
	Good	Poor
1. Study in the library.		
2. Talk on the phone.		
3. Study in bed.		
4. Do school work late at night.		
5. Play music while doing schoolwork.		
6. Study in a noisy place.		
7. Study difficult subjects first.		
8. Study when I am alert and focused.		
9. See my teacher to talk about my work on a regular basis.		
10. Study with friends.		

▷ Compare answers with other students. You don't have to agree, but you should explain the reasons for your answers.

▶Exploring and Understanding Reading

Previewing

Writers use different types of headings and different types of graphics (for example, numbers or asterisks) to help the reader get important information quickly. Some parts of the reading are in **boldface** or *italics*. By previewing special parts of the reading, you can get a quick idea of the topic of a reading.

◗ Looking quickly at special parts of the reading such as graphics (pictures or drawings), titles (headings in **boldface** and *italics*), and subtitles (headings in italics), is previewing. As you preview, you can get a quick idea of the topic of a reading. As you preview, ask yourself these questions:

1. What kind of information will I learn from this reading?
2. What is the overall topic of this reading?
3. Who would be interested in this information?

◗ Compare your answers with a partner.

Time Management for Academic Success

To be successful in school, the first task is to try to guess how much time it will take you to get the work done and get it done well. The general rule is two–three hours of work for every class hour you have. To use your time well, you should make a schedule.

To help you schedule your time, follow these time management techniques about what to do, when to do it, how to do it, and what not to do. As you read, underline, circle, or otherwise note the suggestions you think you can use.

When to Study

Be aware of the time of the day that is best for you. Many people learn best during the daytime. If this is true for you, schedule study time or your most difficult subjects when the sun is up.

Many successful business people begin the day at 5 A.M. or earlier. Athletes and people who practice meditation use this time too. Some writers complete their best work before 9 A.M.

Some people experience the same benefits by staying up late. They work best after midnight.

If you aren't sure what's best for you, experiment. When you need to study, get up early or stay up late.

Where to Study

Use a regular study area. Your body and your mind both react to where you are. When you use the same place to study, day after day, they become trained. When you arrive at that particular place, you can focus your attention more quickly.

Study when you'll be alert. In bed, your body gets a signal. For most students, it's "Time to sleep" and not "Time to study"! For that reason, don't sleep where you study. Just as you train your body to be alert at your desk, you also train it to slow down near your bed.

Easy chairs and sofas are also dangerous places to study.

Use a library. Libraries are designed for learning. The lighting is perfect. The noise level is low. Materials are available. Most people can get more done in a shorter time at the library. Experiment for yourself.

Ways to Handle the Rest of the World

Get off the phone. Your cell phone can be the worst problem. It has the greatest power to interrupt us. People who wouldn't think of bothering you might call at the worst times because they can't see that you are studying. If a simple "I can't talk, I'm studying" doesn't work, then turn your phone off or unplug it. Get an answering machine and let it pick up your calls, or study at the library.

Learn to say no. This is a time saver and a valuable life skill for everyone. Many people feel it is impolite or even rude and insulting to refuse a request. But saying no can be done effectively and politely.

Avoid noise distractions. Don't study in front of the television and turn off the music. Many students insist that they study better with background noises, and that may be true. Some students report good results with certain types of music, such as classical or jazz. However, a majority of research indicates that silence is the best form of music for study.

Schedule study sessions for times when your living environment is usually quiet. If you live in a residence hall, ask if study rooms are available. Or go somewhere else where it's quiet, such as the library. Some students even study in quiet restaurants, cafés, laundromats, and churches.

Things You Can Ask Yourself When You Get Stuck

Ask: Can I do just one more thing? Ask yourself this question at the end of a long day. Almost always you will have enough energy to do just one more short task. The overall increase in the amount of work you can get done might surprise you.

Understanding Details

◗ Answer in note form as completely as possible. Underline the words in the reading that support your answer.

1. What does the author suggest you do while you read?

   _____

2. When is the best time for people to study?

   _____

3. Why is it important to choose a particular place to study?

   _____

4. What places does the author recommend?

   _____

5. What are three things to avoid doing when you have to study?

   a. _____

   b. _____

   c. _____

◗ Compare answers with a partner. Look back at the reading if you disagree.

Note Taking

▷ **Listing Key Words and Phrases** Choose two of the study suggestions that you are interested in. List in note form the important information (i.e., the steps, benefits, or reasons) for the suggestions you chose. Look at the example below to see how to make notes. Notice the key words and phrases. Compare these notes to the information in the reading.

Example: Use a library
1. good lighting
2. low noise level
3. materials available
4. get work done more quickly

A. _____   B. _____

1. _____   1. _____

2. _____   2. _____

3. _____   3. _____

4. _____   4. _____

5. _____   5. _____

Talking About the Information

▷ **1.** Work with a partner who wrote about one of the same suggestions as you. Compare your notes orally.

2. Work with a partner who prepared notes for a different suggestion and take turns explaining the information to each other.

Evaluating the Information

▷ Complete the information below. Then, share your ideas with a partner or in a small group.

From the reading and your experience, what study techniques do you think are the most difficult, the easiest, the least effective, and the most effective for you to use?

1. Most difficult _____

2. Easiest _____

3. Least effective _____

4. Most effective _____

▷ Make a list of two or three techniques you agree in your group are the most important or effective. Present your group's choices to the class and explain the reasons for your choices.

Applying the Information

▶ **Problem Solving** Think of three study problems that make it hard for you to succeed in your courses, for example, completing homework assignments.

▶ **1.** a. List your study problems separately on a piece of paper.

   b. Give your papers to the teacher.

2. a. Form small groups for problem solving.

   b. Your teacher will give each group a set number of problems to solve.

   c. Together, discuss solutions to the problems you were given.

   d. Report your problems and solutions to the class.

▶ Vocabulary Building

Word Form and Meaning

▶ **A** Match the words in Column A with their meanings in Column B.

Column A

_____ 1. connect

_____ 2. contribute

_____ 3. participate

_____ 4. react

_____ 5. research

Column B

a. to study or investigate something

b. to attach something or someone to another

c. to give aid or help with something

d. to join in or take part in something

e. to answer to or behave in response to something

▶ **B** Study these five words and their forms: verb, noun, adjective, and adverb. Then choose the correct form for each part of speech in the chart on the next page. These words are commonly found in general and academic texts.

connect (v.)	contribute (v.)	participate (v.)	react (v.)	research (v.)
connection (n.)	contribution	participant	reaction	research
connector (n.)	contributing	participation	reactive	researched
connecting (adj.)	contributory	participating	reactor	researcher
connected (adj.)	contributor		reactively	
connectedly (adv.)				

Verb	Noun	Adjective	Adverb
contribute	1.	1.	
	2.	2.	
participate	1.	1.	
	2.		
react	1.	1.	1.
	2.		
research	1.	1.	
	2.		

▶ Compare lists with a partner. Try to agree on the same answers.

▶ **C** Write three or more sentences using words from the list.

▶ **D Verbs: Present and Past** Write the past form of the following verbs. Circle these past tense verbs in the reading.

1. ask   _____

2. compare   _____

3. decide   _____

4. feel   _____

5. help   _____

6. improve   _____

7. involve   _____

8. make   _____

9. spend   _____

10. understand _____

▶ Check your answers. Write three sentences and three questions of your own, using both the present and past forms of any of these verbs.

Vocabulary in Context

◗ **A** When you don't know the meaning of a new word, you can use the words you know to help you make a good guess. Use your understanding of the words or phrases in boldface to help you guess the word that is missing.

◗ Complete each sentence with one of the following words.

a. arrive   b. ask   c. complete   d. discover   e. experiment
f. increase   g. lose   h. schedule   i. surprise   j. train

1. I studied at the library **for the first time** and was happy to _____ that I could do all my homework quickly.

2. It will _____ you **to find out** how much more you can do when you study early in the morning.

3. She had many **questions** that she wanted to _____ .

4. She had to _____ all the work **before she could go home**.

5. My friend was late and I **waited over an hour** for him to _____ at the library.

6. I'll **check my calendar** to see if we can _____ a time to get together and finish the project.

7. I decided to _____ by **getting up at different times** until I found the best time to study.

8. It takes **time and willpower** to _____ yourself not to answer the phone when it rings.

9. The **answering machine is on** to take my calls. I don't want to _____ study time talking on the phone.

10. You can _____ the amount of work you get done by **getting up fifteen minutes earlier than you normally would every day**.

◗ Work with a partner and take turns reading the completed sentences.

◗ **B** Often a word has the same form when it is used as a noun and as a verb. Look at the following sentences and indicate if the word in boldface is used as a noun or as a verb. Mark *N* or *V* on the line provided.

1. _____ You might need to **schedule** an appointment with your advisor.

2. _____ I wanted to complete this **experiment** before making a recommendation.

3. _____ The problem was new so a lot of **research** was needed before we could begin to look at how to solve it.

4. _____ I never had the **experience** of studying for an exam so I decided to join a study group.

5. _____ The **practice** was very useful and definitely contributed to my success.

6. _____ The phone has the greatest **power** to interrupt and disturb people.

▶ Write a sentence of your own using the other form (noun or verb) of the words used in the sentences above.

▶ **C Sentence Form** Tips are often written in the form of a command to do or not do something. The sentence usually begins with a verb. Scan the readings and find five sentences that start with a verb and give suggestions or commands.

    Example: <u>Practice</u> these new time management techniques.
                 verb

▶ Write the sentence. Underline the verb.

1. _____

2. _____

3. _____

4. _____

5. _____

▶ Work with a partner and take turns reading your sentences.

❯Expanding Your Language

Reading

 Reading Tip

Guessing what information you'll find out about **before reading** is an important critical reading skill to develop. ■

This reading builds on the ideas introduced in the first reading. It is a short report on research about habits that relate to academic success. You may notice how much easier it is to understand the ideas now that you have some ideas on the topic.

▶ What kind of information would you expect to find in an article that gives advice based on research that experts have carried out? Check (✔) the items you expect to find in the reading from the following list.

_____ Tips (Do's and Don'ts)

_____ Facts about how the research was done

_____ Details (facts) of the results (what was learned) from the research

_____ Interviews with the people that researchers talked to

_____ Short stories about different people's experiences

_____ Long stories about different people's experiences

_____ Details that explain the reasons for the report

▶ Compare your choices with your partner's. Try to agree on your answers.

Harvard University's Habits for Success

❶   Many different types of self-help books advise the reader to develop the skills, goals, and attitudes that will both promote success and provide for a healthy lifestyle. Now, after interviewing 1,600 university students, researchers at Harvard University in Boston, Massachusetts, have found out what contributed both to their academic success and their feeling of satisfaction.

❷   What they found out is so important that the university decided to make changes to its policies. Some examples of the changes it has made are giving more group homework and scheduling classes later in the day. The purpose of these changes is to encourage students to continue talking about their classes over dinner.

❸   How did the researchers get their information? First they asked a lot of questions. They asked about everything, from what students did in their free time to the quality of the teaching and the advising. Researchers looked for patterns to find what made some courses useful. They asked the students about their feelings—if they were happy or satisfied or excited about what they were learning. Then they compared the answers they got to the students' success in their courses. The purpose of their questions was to find out what made the students happy and what helped them learn.

❹   Here are a few of the tips from their research:

- *Get to know your professor.* Each semester students take classes from four or five professors. Get to know at least one of these professors and have them get to know you. This helps a student to feel connected to the school. Another important tip is to ask for advice from your professor about the course work you do. Ask specific questions about what you need to do to improve. For example, questions such as, "How can I make my argument in the first paragraph more effective?" are the best for getting the advice you need. The study showed that most of the students who asked for help improved their grades, while those who didn't got a bad grade or failed.

- *Study in groups.* Doing homework is important but it's not always enough. In order to really understand the ideas, it's better to meet with a small group of two or three students after you study. Complete the assignments with them. Those students who did this understood the information better. They felt more connected to the class, and participated more in their classes.

- *Allow enough time to do a good job.* Those in the Harvard study who did well at school spent more time studying than those who did not. Those students who succeeded studied for two to three hours without interruptions. Those who did not do as well only studied for twenty to thirty minutes at a time at certain times of the day, such as before dinner or after a sports practice. Very few students are aware of this need for uninterrupted study time.

- *Join an activity.* You might not realize how important it is to join a club or a team, but it is. You don't have to be a great athlete to join a club. Even students without special talents can help out in a sports club by helping the team coach. You can help by doing jobs like preparing water bottles or getting oranges cut up for people to eat during games and practices. Students who got involved in an activity—even in a small way—felt more positive about their education.

❺   You can manage your time so that you will be successful in your studies. And, if you make a schedule and keep to it, you can have fun and enjoy yourself with the students in your classes. When you make time to work hard and leave time to play hard, you will succeed. The feeling of happiness that comes with success is the result of following this advice.

From "The Harvard Guide to Happiness"

True or False?   ▷ Answer the following questions based on the reading. Correct any information that is false.

1. T F   If students say they feel happy at school, it doesn't tell us if students will be successful or not.

2. T F   For many years Harvard University has known what students should do to succeed in their classes.

3. T F   It is important to ask your professor a general question such as "How can I get a better grade?"

4. T F   Students should work in groups to complete homework assignments.

5. T F   Many students know that it's important to have uninterrupted study time in order to do well in school.

6. T F   Students who participate in school activities feel more positive about their school.

Writing   ▷ **Topic Writing** Write about some study habits that are important to you based on your discussion and the chapter readings.
    To do this, follow these steps.

▷ **1.** Outline the ideas about each habit.

Study Habit 1: _____   Study Habit 2: _____

What _____   What _____

How _____   How _____

_____   _____

_____   _____

Why _____   Why _____

_____   _____

_____   _____

2. Write two or three sentences about *the habit*.

3. Write three or four sentences about *how* to follow it.

4. Write three or four sentences about *why* it is important.

5. Write about each habit in a separate paragraph.

◐ In writing, remember to do the following:

- Indent at the beginning of the paragraph, as in this example:

    There are three main study techniques that I think are important for being successful in school.

- Explain the ideas in complete sentences. In English, a sentence usually has a subject, a verb, and an object.

    <u>Many students</u> <u>get</u> <u>an answering machine</u>.
    subject   verb   object

Online Study Center   For additional activities, go to the *Reading Matters* Online Study Center at *college.hmco.com/pic/wholeytwo2e.*

② Habits of a Lifetime: Are We Affected?

▶ Chapter Openers

Discussion Questions

▶ **Lifestyles** Think about these questions. Share your ideas with a partner or in a small group.

1. a. What habits can lead to a long life?

   b. What habits might shorten your life?

2. Are people's lives today easier or more difficult than they were in the past?

3. How would your life change without modern conveniences such as indoor plumbing or electricity?

▶ Paired Readings

In this section, you will find two different stories on the same theme. Choose one of the two to work with. Prepare to explain the story to someone who read the same story and then to a person who read the other story.

▶ These are the stories of two women who have lived long and interesting lives. Imagine you were preparing to meet someone who was much older than you and who had lived through difficult times. What would you expect them to tell you?

Predicting

▶ Write (in a few words) what you expect to read about in this story. List as many ideas as you can. The first idea is given as an example.

I expect to read about…

1. remembrance of historical events

2. _____

3. _____

4. _____

5. _____

❶A Life Well Lived

Understanding Details

▷ Read the story and then look for the answers to the questions after each paragraph. Underline the words in the paragraph that support your answers.

The Road Less Traveled

Eighty-seven-year-old Birdle Mannon

❶   Birdle Mannon is eighty-seven and lives in a one-room wood house built by her father in the woods near the village of Brownbranch, forty miles away from Springfield, Missouri. She doesn't have electricity, running water, or indoor plumbing. She heats her house and cooks her food on a wood stove that she keeps supplied by cutting her own wood. She collects rainwater to use for cooking, bathing, and washing her clothes. When she needs to, she uses an outhouse that she built down the path from her house. She cooks her own food from a few supplies that she buys in the village. She keeps food cold in a special underground cellar next to her house. The year is 1997 but her life is not very different from the way it was when she first came to this place with her family in 1916.

1. Where does Birdle Mannon live?

   _____

2. How does Birdle heat her home?

   _____

3. Where does she get her water?

   _____

4. When did she first come to her home?

   _____

5. How are her home and her life similar to the way they were when she first came there?

   a. _____

   b. _____

   c. _____

   d. _____

   e. _____

---

❷   Birdle came to Missouri with her parents, her brother, and two sisters in 1916. They came because they heard that there was good land and lots of water available for farming. Mr. Mannon bought 120 acres of land for $800. It was autumn when the family arrived and Birdle's father quickly built a tiny wood house for protection before winter arrived. Birdle remembers sleeping on the

floor while the house was being built. The family was poor. Birdle's father worked hard to raise crops like corn and oats, chickens, and cattle to survive. Times were not easy. One of Birdle's sisters died in the flu epidemic of 1918. Her brother died in 1926 and her father died in 1936. The Mannons acquired only a few modern conveniences. They had a pick-up truck, a portable radio, and in 1970, they got a telephone installed. After her mother died in 1969 and her sister in 1972, Birdle was left alone and had to manage on her own.

1. Why did Birdle's family come to Brownbranch, Missouri?

   _____

2. a. How much land did Birdle's father buy?

   _____

   b. How much did the land cost?

   _____

3. What did Birdle's father do to support the family?

   _____

4. What happened to Birdle's family?

   _____

5. What happened to Birdle after 1972?

   _____

❸   Birdle decided to stay in her house in the woods, but not because she didn't have other opportunities in life. She had gone to college and trained to be a teacher. She taught school in two of the villages near her home. She also taught Sunday school at the local church and wrote local news reports for two area newspapers. Birdle chose to stay in her home because, as she says, "This is the place where I belong." Birdle's attitude is that a person can't do everything in life, so do what makes you happy. She may not have an easy life, but she has kept busy. Some people in the community worry that at eighty-seven Birdle is too old to be living by herself. Usually, her neighbors try to help her. They stop in to bring her to the village store for groceries or to bring her to church on Sunday. Birdle is glad for the assistance from her neighbors but she's not yet ready to leave her house in the woods. As she says, "I can still cut my own wood and pump my own water. In my mind and heart, I don't feel old." She is living proof of the saying "Old habits die hard."

1. What facts show that Birdle could have lived a different kind of life?

_____

_____

2. What is her attitude toward life?

_____

_____

3. Why do Birdle's neighbors worry about her?

_____

_____

4. How does Birdle feel about living in the woods at her age?

_____

_____

▶ Compare answers with your partner. Try to agree on the same answers. Look back at the reading if you disagree.

Recapping the Story

▶ Work with a partner who read the same story. Reread the first paragraph quickly. Cover the information and tell your partner as much as you can remember. Ask for help if you forget or give incorrect information. Take turns reading and telling the information in all the paragraphs.

Reacting to the Story

▶ Discuss these questions with a partner.

1. a. Would you ever choose to live the way Birdle does?
   b. What would you like about it, and what would you miss?
2. Do you think that Birdle can continue to live on her own? Why or why not?
3. Do you agree with Birdle's attitude toward life? Why or why not?

❷The Secrets of a Long Life

Understanding Details

▶ Read the story and then look for the answers to the questions after each paragraph. Underline the words in the paragraph that support your answers.

A Positive Approach to Life

❶ Jeanne Calment holds the record for being one of the world's oldest people. When she died in 1997, she was 122 years of age. Many people were curious about this unusual woman. Reporters asked her about her memories. Calment could remember meeting the painter, Vincent Van Gogh, at a local grocery store in 1888. She told reporters that she thought he was a grouchy and disagreeable man. A lawyer made a deal with her in 1965 when she was 90 years old. He agreed to pay her $500 a month rent on an apartment she owned if it would become his when she died. He died at age 77 in

Jeanne Calment lived 122 years.

December of 1995 after paying her $180,000, twice the value of the apartment. Calment joked about this saying, "We all make bad deals in life." Reporters often asked her to tell them the secret of her long life. She would just shrug and say, "Maybe God has forgotten me." People asked her a lot of questions about the details of her daily life. Perhaps they hoped that they could find the key to living a long and active life by finding out about her daily habits.

1. Who was Jeanne Calment?

_____

2. When did she die?

_____

3. a. How did she meet Vincent Van Gogh?

_____

b. What did she think of him?

_____

4. What deal did she make for her apartment?

_____

5. What did people ask her about?

a. _____

b. _____

6. Why did people want to know about the details of her life?

_____

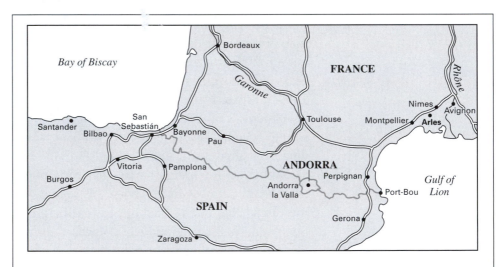

❷   Jeanne lived in Arles, a city in southern France, where she was born in 1875. She was born into a middle-class family and lived an ordinary life. She married and had a daughter. Unfortunately, her husband, her daughter, and an only grandson all died before her, leaving her to live alone. Her eating habits were not especially healthy. She ate chocolate almost every day. In fact, she once estimated that she ate about a kilogram of chocolate a week. She liked to smoke and she smoked cigarettes until she was 117 years old. She also liked to drink a glass of wine with her noon meal. She took care of her physical appearance, regularly rubbing her skin with olive oil. She was an active woman and rode a bicycle until she was 100 years old. She took a brisk, long walk every day. On her 100th birthday, she even walked all over the city to thank different people for wishing her a happy birthday.

1. Where did Jeanne spend her life?

_____

2. What sad events happened in her life?

_____

3. What habits did she have?

    a. _____

    b. _____

    c. _____

    d. _____

4. What kind of physical activities did she like?

    a. _____

    b. _____

❸   Many people asked Calment to tell them her secrets for living a long life. Certainly, her family history must have played some part; her mother lived to be 86 and her father lived to be 93. But, people who knew Calment suggest that the secret lies in the makeup of her personality. Friends said that she didn't seem to worry too much. She didn't appear to suffer from stress. She had a positive approach toward life. She said, "If you can't do anything about it, don't worry about it." She was the kind of person who looked for things in life to smile about. At the age of 114, she acted in a film about Van Gogh and made a film about herself and a CD of her music. In her later years she couldn't see or hear people because she had become deaf and blind. In spite of that, she still felt that she had something to be happy about every day.

1. What was important about Jeanne Calment's family history?

_____

2. What was her approach toward life?

_____

3. a. What physical problems did Jeanne have?

_____

   b. How did they affect her attitude toward life?

_____

▶ Compare answers with your partner. Try to agree on the same answers. Look back at the reading if you disagree.

Recapping the Story

▶ Reread the first paragraph quickly. Cover the information and tell your partner as much as you can remember. Ask for help if you forget or give incorrect information. Take turns reading and telling the information in all the paragraphs.

Reacting to the Story

▶ Share your ideas about these questions with a partner.

1. What do you find interesting about this woman's life?
2. What habits do you think helped this woman to live a long life?
3. What do you think is the secret to living a long life?

▶Comparing the Readings

Discussing the Stories

▷ **A** Work with a partner (or partners) who read a different story. Tell your partner the details of the story you read. Then, listen to your partner's story. Discuss the similarities and differences between these stories.

▷ **B** Discuss the questions in the "Reacting to the Story" section for both stories.

▷ **C** Make a list. What are the lessons for living long and fulfilling lives in these two readings? Be prepared to share your list with others in the class.

Giving Your Opinion

▷ What do you think has the greatest influence on our chances for a long and fulfilling life? List five things that influence our chances to live long and happy lives. List your ideas from most (1) to least (5) important.

Example: positive attitude

1. _____

2. _____

3. _____

4. _____

5. _____

▷ Work with a partner or in a small group. Try to agree on the factors and, if possible, on their order of importance. Report the results to your classmates.

▶Vocabulary Building

Word Form and Meaning

▷ **A** Match the words in Column A with their meanings in Column B.

Column A

_____ 1. acquire

_____ 2. approach

_____ 3. avail

_____ 4. collect

_____ 5. estimate

Column B

a. to guess or judge something

b. to gather together

c. to get or gain something

d. to come close or near to someone or something

e. to use or be helped by someone

▶ **B** Study these five words and their forms: verb, noun, adjective, and adverb. Then choose the correct form for each part of speech in the chart below. These words are commonly found in general and academic texts.

acquire (v.)	approach (v.)	avail (v.)	collect (v.)	estimate (v.)
acquisition (n.)	approaching	available	collector	estimate
acquired (adj.)	approachable	availability	collection	estimation
acquisitive (adj.)	approachability	availably	collected	estimated
acquisitively (adv.)	approach		collectable	

Verb	Noun	Adjective	Adverb
approach	1.	1.	
	2.	2.	
avail	1.	1.	1.
collect	1.	1.	
	2.	2.	
estimate	1.	1.	
	2.		

▶ Compare lists with a partner. Try to agree on the same answers.

▶ **C** Write three or more sentences using words from the list.

▶ **D Synonyms** Circle the word that is closest in meaning to the boldface word.

1. **heat** make prepare warm serve
2. **protection** safety building floor supplies
3. **produce** provide make speak use
4. **curious** glad active questioning ready
5. **attitude** outlook habit proof opportunity
6. **active** happy physical busy passive
7. **blind** unhearing unseeing unbelieving unusual
8. **brisk** slow sudden fast poor

▶ Write three or more sentences using words from the list.

▶ **E Antonyms** Antonyms are two words that have opposite meanings, like *good* and *bad*. Match the word in Column A with its antonym in Column B.

Column A

_____ 1. happy

_____ 2. quickly

_____ 3. positive

_____ 4. smile

_____ 5. different

_____ 6. near

_____ 7. old

_____ 8. long

_____ 9. remember

_____ 10. usual

Column B

a. unusual

b. negative

c. short

d. slowly

e. forget

f. frown

g. similar

h. young

i. sad

j. far

▶ Write three or more sentences using words from the list.

Vocabulary in Context

Often, when you read, you'll notice that an idea is followed by **details about that idea**. You can use the examples or details to help you understand the general idea better. ■

Refer to the readings to help make your choices in the vocabulary activities. ■

▶ **General Ideas and Specific Facts** In English, a general idea given in one sentence of part of a sentence is often followed by sentences that contain specific facts about—or examples of—that general idea.

Match each general sentence in Column A with one with details from Column B that best follows.

Column A

_____ 1. They acquired only a few modern conveniences.

_____ 2. Her neighbors try to help her.

_____ 3. Her eating habits were not especially healthy.

_____ 4. She took care of her physical appearance.

Column B

a. They stop in to bring her to the village store for groceries or to bring her to church on Sunday.

b. She regularly rubbed her skin with olive oil.

c. They had a pick-up truck, a portable radio, and they got a telephone.

d. She ate chocolate almost every day. In fact, she once estimated that she ate about a kilogram of chocolate a week.

▶ Work with a partner to read the pairs of sentences. Look for other sentences in the readings that follow this pattern of general informaton followed by specific facts.

Expanding Your Language

Reading   ▶ This reading expands on the idea of health habits. Notice how much easier it is to understand this now that you have done some reading beforehand. First, read the following questions. After reading, answer them based on the information in the text.

1. What are companies trying to encourage their employees to do?
2. What alarming facts has the Federal Department of Health and Human Services published?
3. What steps has Union Pacific Railroad taken to improve workers' health?
4. Why are the elevators in Sprint's brand new headquarters slow?
5. What has Sprint done to encourage people to change their parking habits?
6. What reaction did employees first have to Sprint's policies?
7. What has been the result of Sprint's efforts to change its employees' habits?

Healthy Habits—The Company Way

Across the United States, companies, states, and even schools are becoming more interested in helping their employees to develop healthier habits. Companies are designing programs to fight what health officials say is an alarming increase in cases of obesity and weight-related diseases such as diabetes. According to estimates from the Federal Department of Health and Human Services, being overweight resulted in an estimated expense of $117 billion in 2000 and approximately 300,000 worker deaths a year.

So companies have decided to introduce some changes to the workplace. Take the example of Union Pacific Railroad. It has begun a program of offering weight-loss drugs to its employees. This program is part of a research project to determine how best to encourage weight loss among its employees. At Sprint's new headquarters in Kansas City, some employees noticed that the elevators seemed to move unusually slowly. Says one employee, "We think the company wants to get us to take the stairs." In fact, the employee is right. They used hydraulic elevators, despite the fact that these are slower, and had windows put along the staircases to encourage people to walk rather than ride between floors. Sprint also planned its 200-acre world headquarters with fitness in mind. Cars are not allowed near the headquarters. Employees must park in garages that are far away. That way workers have a walk of approximately half a mile each day.

Will this plan to change habits work? At first, the employees at Sprint didn't follow the plan. The company provided electric buses between the buildings and the parking garages for those who didn't want to walk. Initially, employees took the buses even though walking would have required less time. Then, three months later, demand for the buses dropped so much that the company stopped using them. And the stairs are now especially popular. According to one employee, walking is no longer a problem. "I used to take the elevator even if I was just going up one floor. Now, if it's three floors or less, I walk." It seems that changing old habits can be less painful than one would think.

Speaking

▶ **Two-Minute Taped Talk** Record a two-minute audiotape or audio CD about one of the stories in this chapter. To make your recording, follow these steps:

▶ **1.** Write some notes about the important information in the story.

2. Practice telling the story from your notes. Include as many important facts as possible.

3. Time yourself as you try to speak as clearly and naturally as possible.

4. Record yourself telling the story.

5. Give the tape or CD to your teacher for feedback.

Writing

▶ **Take a Position** In the future, people will live longer. Write your opinion about the following question:

What do you think are the most important things people should do if they want to live a long and fulfilling life?

▶ **1.** Go back to the exercises in the "Comparing the Readings" section on page 23. Use the information from these exercises and the discussions you've had to help focus your ideas.

2. Write a list of ideas. For each idea, think of some facts, examples, stories, or other information of your own as in the example below. Do this work in your journal notebook.

A. To live a long life
    Idea 1: Be active
    • Walk every day (Jeanne Calment)
    •
    Idea 2:
    •
    •

B. To live a fulfilling life
    Idea 1: Have a positive attitude
    • Don't worry about yesterday's problems, do something good today
    •
    Idea 2:
    •
    •

2. Work with a partner and explain your ideas to each other. Help each other to add to the list of ideas.

3. Write your ideas in complete sentences. Indent at the beginning of each paragraph.

4. Give your final writing to your teacher.

Online Study Center For additional activities, go to the *Reading Matters* Online Study Center at *college.hmco.com/pic/wholeytwo2e.*

3 The Power of Naps

Chapter Openers

Discussion Questions

▶ Think about these questions. Share your ideas with a partner or a small group.

1. Do you feel sleepy during the day? At what times?
2. What do you do to "wake up" when you feel sleepy?
3. If you could, would you take a nap during the day?
   a. When?
   b. For how long?
   c. Where?
4. Do you think that taking a nap is a sign of laziness? Why or why not?

Getting Information from a Graph

▶ Use information in the graph to answer the questions on the next page.

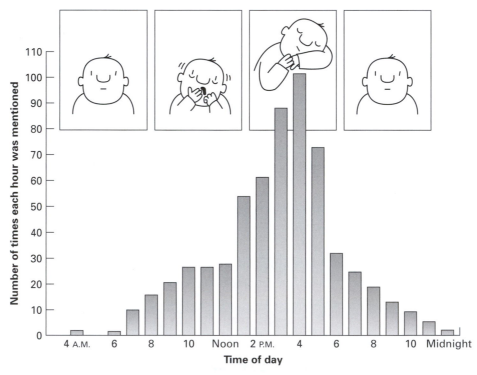

Two hundred seventy-six young adults reported that they feel sleepy most often in the middle of the afternoon.

1. When did people in this study say they felt tired most frequently?

   _____

2. How many times did people say they felt tired at:

   2 P.M. _____

   9 A.M. _____

   6 P.M. _____

3. What could be some reasons more people feel tired at 4 P.M. than at 6 P.M.?

   _____

Exploring and Understanding Reading

Predicting

This reading contains some factual information and advice about our need for sleep. You can more easily understand the reading by thinking about what happens to you when you get tired.

▶ Check (✔) the things that people might do when they feel tired. Add two ideas of your own.

_____ 1. Forget a person's name.

_____ 2. Forget to do something important.

_____ 3. Solve a difficult problem.

_____ 4. Work an extra shift or work overtime.

_____ 5. Make a bad decision.

_____ 6. Get angry with a friend.

_____ 7. _____

_____ 8. _____

▶ Work with a partner to compare your choices.

We Need to Nap!

❶   Do you ever feel sleepy during the day? Sleep researchers have found some interesting facts about our body's natural sleep rhythms. There are two points during a 24-hour period when people most feel the need to sleep. These times are the hours between 1 and 4 P.M. in the afternoon and between 1 and 4 A.M. in the morning. One study of 276 young adults showed that people have the most difficulty staying awake between two and five o'clock in the afternoon and in the morning. These are also the hours when there are increases in traffic accidents causing death. Being tired affects your ability to think and make decisions. You forget more easily and feel less alert. You have slower reaction times. In addition, fatigue affects our mood and outlook on life.

❷   North Americans seem to be cutting down on the number of hours they sleep. In many countries, people stop their work in the afternoon and take a nap. But, in countries such as Canada and the United States, business continues all day long. In North America, the number of people who work for 10–12 hours a day is increasing. More people are working overtime. More people are working night shifts, from 11 P.M. until 7 A.M. But most adults need about 7–10 hours of sleep a day. On average, North Americans are only getting about 6–8 hours of sleep. In fact, over the past century, North Americans have reduced the number of nightly sleeping hours by about twenty percent. These lost hours of sleep have been replaced mainly by work and work-related activities. People have added an extra 158 hours—the equivalent of four work weeks—to their yearly work schedule.

❸   Some experts are worried that tired workers are becoming a danger in the workplace. A tired worker is likely to forget important information and make mistakes. Mistakes can lead to serious work accidents. Tiredness has been linked either directly or indirectly to some of the worst accidents in history, such as the nuclear accident at Three Mile Island and the explosion of the space shuttle, Challenger. Allowing workers to nap could be a helpful response to the the problem. Studies have also shown that an afternoon nap can significantly increase mental abilities and improve mood. Among the mental benefits are the ability to pay attention to a task and the ability to make complicated decisions. Research into allowing people in the airline industry to take short naps is producing some interesting results. Researchers at NASA have studied the effects of taking forty-minute naps for pilots on overseas international flights. They found that when pilots napped, they were more alert afterward and could function better. Their reactions were sixteen times faster than crew members who hadn't napped.

❹　　Sleep researchers have some advice for people who want to make a habit of napping in the afternoon.

What To Do

- Take a nap at the time when your body most needs to sleep: eight hours after getting up and eight hours before your bedtime at night.
- Take a nap every day even if you don't feel tired.
- Remind yourself that taking a nap is not a sign of laziness.
- Find a place to lie down to nap.
- Shut off your phone or close the door so that you won't worry about being disturbed.
- Take a minute to breathe slowly and relax your body before closing your eyes.
- Nap for 15–20 minutes. Try not to nap for longer than 30 minutes.
- After you wake up, move slowly for a few minutes. Don't try to move into action quickly.

Getting the Main Idea

> **Reading Tip**

The **main idea** of a paragraph is the **general idea of the paragraph as a whole**. Ask yourself, "What is the writer trying to explain in this paragraph?" Finding the main idea is an important critical reading strategy. It helps you to see how information in the sentences of the paragraph are related to one general idea. ■

◗　Read the list of main ideas. Write the main idea for each of the paragraphs on the correct line.

Main Ideas

Some advice for people who want to take a nap in the afternoon.
The decrease in the amount of time people are sleeping.
Some information about our body's natural sleep rhythms.
The problem of tired workers and some solutions to this problem.

Paragraph 1. _____

Paragraph 2. _____

Paragraph 3. _____

Paragraph 4. _____

Scanning for Facts

> **Reading Tip**

Scanning is helpful when you want to **answer** a **particular question**. To scan, first read the question. Use **key words** of the question and what you remember from previewing to help you quickly locate the right information in the reading. ■

◗　**A** Circle *T* for true or *F* for false. Underline the information that supports your answer. Correct any information that is false.

1.　T　F　　More people feel tired at 4:00 P.M. than at 10:00 in the morning.

2.　T　F　　There are more traffic accidents at four o'clock than at six o'clock.

3.　T　F　　Fatigue can make people moody.

4.　T　F　　People in the United States and Canada are getting more sleep than in the past.

5.　T　F　　Fatigue causes accidents at work.

▶ **B** Circle the correct choice in each sentence. Underline the information in the reading that supports your answer.

1. In North America people **are** / **aren't** in the habit of taking a nap.

2. In many countries people **do** / **don't** work all day.

3. In North America **more** / **fewer** people are working night shifts.

4. Our bodies have **one** / **two** periods when we feel the need to sleep the most.

5. Many Americans **do** / **don't** feel tired during the day.

6. Naps **increase** / **decrease** mental capacity on the job.

7. Pilots who napped had **faster** / **slower** reactions in carrying out their work.

▶ Compare answers with a partner. Try to agree on the same answers. Look back at the reading if you disagree.

In-Class Survey

▶ Answer these questions for yourself. Interview two others in your class. Write their answers in note form.

1. a. During the day, do you feel tired?

   Often   Sometimes   Never

   b. If you do, at what time of the day do you feel most sleepy?

2. How many hours do you usually sleep?

   4–6   6–8   8–10

3. When do you usually go to bed?

4. When do you usually get up?

5. a. Do you ever take a nap during the day?

   b. If yes, when do you take a nap? For how long?

6. Is it a good idea for people to take naps at work? Explain the reasons for your answer.

   Yes   No

▶ Discuss your answers with a partner. Did people answer the questions similarly or differently?

Applying the Information

▶ Read the short article that follows and then discuss this question: Why are German workers being encouraged to nap?

Who Naps Most?

The European country that naps the most. What country would you think wins that particular prize? Spain, Portugal, or Italy. If you guessed any of these southern European nations, you would be wrong. The correct answer would be Germany. According to a five-year study by American sleep researchers, twenty-two percent of Germans reported napping at least three days a week. Spaniards napped far less frequently. Only seven percent of them reported taking the traditional afternoon nap. Why do Germans feel the need to nap? It may be because they get less sleep at night than the Spanish. Or it may be because they go to bed before 11 P.M. and get up at 6 A.M. By 3 P.M. a German worker has been up for nine hours and needs to take a "power nap."

In fact, the German Institute for Sleep Research reported that afternoon naps were the best way for workers to be at their best and be more alert. As a result, the government decided to have "quiet areas" for civil servants to go to and take a quick nap in the middle of the day. Some private companies have also concluded that this is a good idea. They have prepared special offices with couches and sofa beds so that their workers can benefit from a mid-day snooze.

Understanding Details

▶ Underline any facts in the article that answer the following questions:

1. Who carried out this research into napping in European countries?
2. What two countries are reported on?
3. How does napping in these countries compare?
4. What are the possible reasons why Germans seem to need to nap?

▶ Work with a partner to discuss your answers.

Using Facts to Make a Case

▶ Based on the ideas in the readings of this chapter, discuss the following question:

Should people in the United States be napping during the day or sleeping more at night?

▶ Work with a partner or in a small group and present your ideas. Try to reach agreement. Prepare to present your ideas to others.

▶Vocabulary Building

**Word Form
and Meaning**

▶ **A** Match the words in Column A with their meanings in Column B.

Column A

_____ 1. benefit

_____ 2. conclude

_____ 3. function

_____ 4. link

_____ 5. respond

Column B

a. to do or perform something

b. to gain from or get help from someone or something

c. to end or reach a decision about something

d. to answer or react to something or someone

e. to connect with or be joined with someone or something

▶ **B** Study these five words and their forms, verb, noun, adjective, and adverb. Then choose the correct form for each part of speech in the chart below. These words are commonly found in general and academic texts.

benefit (v.)	conclude (v.)	function (v.)	link (v.)	respond (v.)
beneficiary (n.)	conclusion	function	link	response
benefit (n.)	conclusive	functioning	linking	responding
beneficial (adj.)	concluding	functional	linked	respondent
beneficently (adv.)	conclusively	functionary		responsively
		functionally		responsive

Verb	Noun	Adjective	Adverb
conclude	1.	1.	1.
	2.		
function	1.	1.	1.
	2.	2.	
link	1.	1.	
		2.	
respond	1.	1.	1.
	2.	2.	

▶ Compare lists with a partner. Try to agree on the same answers.

▶ **C** Write three or more sentences using words from the list.

▶ **D** In English, the form of a word can change when it is used as a different part of speech. In these sentences you will decide if you need a *noun* (an idea or a thing) or an *adjective* (a word that describes an idea or a thing).

▶ Choose the correct word to complete the sentences.

1. sleep / sleepy

   a. My need for _____ was affecting my ability to get my work done.

   b. I felt _____ even though I had gone to bed at 9:00 P.M.

2. mood / moody

   a. She didn't like to be with him when he was _____.

   b. He didn't want to stay because she was in a bad _____.

3. day / daily

   a. I work eight hours every _____, six days a week.

   b. Her _____ routine was always changing.

4. difficulty / difficult

   a. It's _____ to concentrate when you feel tired.

   b. She had _____ with the schedule.

5. night / nightly

   a. She liked her _____ routine of reading the newspapers.

   b. She didn't like to work at _____ because she felt tired the next day.

▶ Work with a partner and take turns reading the completed sentences.

▶ **E Matching Meanings** Match the word in Column A with its meaning in Column B.

Column A	Column B
_____ 1. continue	a. stop for a period of time
_____ 2. alert	b. response to an action
_____ 3. benefit	c. go on for a period of time
_____ 4. reduce	d. advantage
_____ 5. surprise	e. decrease
_____ 6. suspend	f. feeling awake and lively
_____ 7. fatigue	g. feeling inactive
_____ 8. lazy	h. the study of a problem
_____ 9. reaction	i. feeling of tiredness
_____10. research	j. without warning

◗Expanding Your Language

Reading   This reading explores a new idea on the subject of sleep habits. Notice how much easier it is to understand this now that you have done some reading on the topic.

▶ First, read the following questions. After reading, answer them based on the information in the text.

1. What is one example that shows New York is "the city that never sleeps"?
2. What is happening that could change the image of New York City as a place where things are open all night?
3. What reason is given for the government's plan to require bars and restaurants to close at 1 A.M.?
4. What are two qualities that make Tokyo so special?
5. What example shows that Tokyo could be called "the city that never sleeps"?

The City That Never Sleeps

"The City That Never Sleeps" has for years been the unofficial title for New York City. With its open-all-night services, New York is alive. If, for example, you want to play hockey at four in the morning, there's an ice rink at 23rd and Hudson that is open twenty-four hours a day. But, lately, club and restaurant owners are worried that New York is trying to get people into the habit of going to bed early. First, a law was passed making it illegal for smokers to light up inside public places. That forced many people to smoke outside. Then, the city government suggested making a law that would close clubs and bars that allow dancing and loud music at 1 A.M. instead of 4 A.M. The city's argument is that it has had an increased number of noise complaints from neighbors who are in the habit of going to bed at midnight. If the city government has its way, then it will have to give up its title to Tokyo.

Morning, noon, and night, seven days a week, twenty-four hours a day, Tokyo is alive. The government has put up signs in public with one word—ambition—to show what drives this city. But, even though Tokyo is busy, respect rules its city streets. Even at the most crowded hours of the day and evening, people never feel jostled, pushed, or crushed. The waves of people crowding the streets exhibit the greatest sense of order and purpose. Tokyo is a city that stays up late and gets up early. At 5 A.M. the Tsukiji fish market is already in action. The market covers one square city block and it is always very full. There are hundreds upon hundreds of people packed into it. At 5:15 the fish sellers ring their bells and begin their bargaining. In five minutes, hundreds of fresh fish have been sold. Tokyo is a city of twelve million people on the move.

Speaking

▶ **A Tell and Retell** Quickly reread the tips on page 31 for what to do if you want to take a nap. Work with a partner. Cover the information and take turns giving as many tips as you can remember to each other.

▶ **B Two-Minute Taped Talk** What are your sleep habits? Have they changed in the last few years? Do you need to get more sleep or are you getting enough? Do you ever feel sleepy?

Using your own ideas and the information in this chapter, prepare a two-minute talk about these questions or any of your own ideas on the topic of sleep and naps. Prepare your ideas before you record. Make a short outline of your ideas in note form. Practice your talk a few times before you record. Record your talk and give it to your teacher for feedback on content and clarity of ideas.

Writing   ▶ **Topic Writing** Write about the topic of your taped talk. Follow the instructions on pages 12 and 13.

❯Read On: Taking It Further

Researchers have found that the more you read, the more your vocabulary will increase and the more you will understand. A good knowledge of vocabulary will help you to do well in school and in business. To find out more about your reading habits, answer the following questionnaire.

Reading Questionnaire

▶ Rank the activities that you think help you to increase the amount of vocabulary you understand. Mark (1) beside those that help you the most to learn new vocabulary, (2) beside the second most helpful, and so on. Mark the same number if you find two activities that help you equally.

_____ Memorizing word lists

_____ Reading texts that are assigned for class

_____ Reading texts that I choose for myself

_____ Talking about the texts that we read for class

_____ Talking about the texts that I choose for myself

_____ Learning how to guess the meaning of words that are new

_____ Doing vocabulary exercises for reading that we study in class

_____ Doing extra vocabulary exercises for homework

_____ Studying the dictionary to find out the parts of words

_____ Using the dictionary to look up new words I don't understand

▶ Discuss your questionnaire with a partner. Do not worry if your answers are different from your partner's. Explain the reasons for your ranking and your experiences with reading. Are there other activities you've found that help you to increase your vocabulary?

Reading Journal

Keep a notebook to write your reading journal and vocabulary log entries. ■

An important way to improve your reading skills and increase your vocabulary is to find material that you choose to read. This activity is called "reading for pleasure." Here are some ideas to start you out.

▶ **A Reading** Find some readings on the topics in this unit that you are interested in and that are at your level. For example, you could find an easy reading edition of "Rip Van Winkle" by Washington Irving. This is the story of a man who took a very long nap. Another source of reading material is your bookstore or library's magazine and newspaper section. Make a schedule for a time when you plan to do your personal reading. Discuss what you would like to read with your teacher and with others in a small group. Your teacher can help you to find some material to read for your pleasure. Your group members could also recommend something good for you to read.

▶ **B Writing** At the end of each week complete a journal report about what you read. Explain the important ideas and what you learned from this reading. Write about what you liked or found interesting. Explain whether or not you would recommend the reading to others.

▶ Include the following information in your journal entry:

Title of the reading: _____

Author: _____

Subject of the reading:

_____

_____

_____

_____

Summary of the important ideas:

_____

_____

_____

_____

Your opinion:

_____

_____

_____

_____

Recommendation:

_____

_____

_____

▶ **C Speaking** Each week, be ready to talk about what you read with a partner or with others in a small group. You can use your journal report to help you to recall what is important for the others to know.

Vocabulary Log

▶ **A** Choose five important words that you learned in each chapter. Write the words and your definition in your notebook as in the example below. Check your definition with the teacher.

Chapter 1

Word	Definition
1. manage	to direct or handle something
2.	
3.	
4.	
5.	

▶ **B Personal Dictionary** A personal dictionary is a good way to record the new words you learn as you read. To create your dictionary, divide a notebook into sections for each letter of the alphabet. Then, write the word and the definition on the appropriate page. You can also write the way to use the word in a sentence (as a verb, as a noun, as an adjective, as an adverb, or in more than one way). Look for the word in the reading or write the word in a sentence of your own. You can also find synonyms (words that mean the same) or antonyms (words that have an opposite meaning) and write them in your dictionary.

Word Play

▶ **A Spelling Game** You can use vocabulary from the chapter readings to play this game. Think of a pair of words, like *paid* and *distract*. The last letter of *paid* is the first letter of *distract*. Select a partner and follow these rules to play the game.

▶ **1.** Make a list of seven to ten words from the readings that can be paired with another word.

2. Give your partner the first word to spell.

3. Your partner spells the word and then must select a new word that begins with the last letter of the word spelled (time limit: one minute). If your partner can't find a word, you supply an answer.

4. Continue to take turns until the teacher calls time (after approximately ten to fifteen minutes).

5. The person who correctly chooses and spells the most words wins.

 ***Online Study Center*** For additional activities, go to the ***Reading Matters*** Online Study Center at *college.hmco.com/pic/wholeytwo2e.*

Exploring Our Roots

If the roots are solid, the tree will grow strong.

—*S. Weil*

Introducing the Topic

In this unit you will read about one of the fastest-growing interests in America—genealogy. Looking into our family history is the third most popular hobby in the United States. Chapter 4 is about the customs and traditions of choosing names. Chapter 5 explores the reasons that people decide to research their roots. In Chapter 6 you will read about autobiographical writing and find out why people write about their own personal history.

◗Points of Interest

Discussion Questions

◗ **Family History** Think about these questions. Share your ideas with a partner or in a small group.

1. Who are the members of your family? What interesting stories do you know about your family or about families in your country?
2. Did you ever try to find out about the past history of your family? If yes, what did you learn? If no, what would you like to learn?
3. Why is it important to tell family stories from one generation to the next?

Family Tree

▶ Complete as much of this chart as you can, adding date and place where each person was born, married, or died, if applicable. Show the chart to a partner and use it to talk about some of the people in your family. If possible, bring photographs of family members.

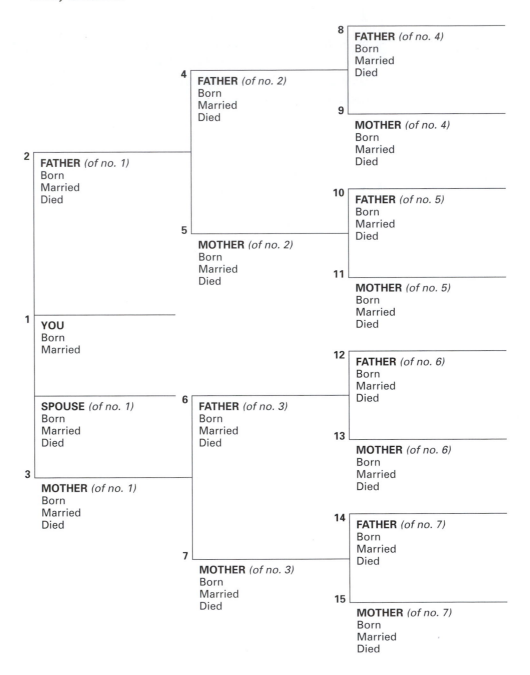

8 FATHER (of no. 4)
Born
Married
Died

4 FATHER (of no. 2)
Born
Married
Died

9 MOTHER (of no. 4)
Born
Married
Died

2 FATHER (of no. 1)
Born
Married
Died

10 FATHER (of no. 5)
Born
Married
Died

5 MOTHER (of no. 2)
Born
Married
Died

11 MOTHER (of no. 5)
Born
Married
Died

1 YOU
Born
Married

12 FATHER (of no. 6)
Born
Married
Died

6 FATHER (of no. 3)
Born
Married
Died

13 MOTHER (of no. 6)
Born
Married
Died

3 SPOUSE (of no. 1)
Born
Married
Died

MOTHER (of no. 1)
Born
Married
Died

14 FATHER (of no. 7)
Born
Married
Died

7 MOTHER (of no. 3)
Born
Married
Died

15 MOTHER (of no. 7)
Born
Married
Died

4 What's in a Name?

▶ Chapter Openers

Discussion Questions

▷ **What's in a Name?** Think about these questions. Share your ideas with a partner or in a small group.

1. What is the origin or meaning of your first name?
2. What do you know about the history of your family name?
3. Would you ever change your name or take a new name? What are some reasons why people change their names or take new names?
4. What names do you like?
5. What are some common nicknames that you know? Do you think nicknames are positive or negative?
6. Is a company's brand name important or not?

▶ Exploring and Understanding Reading

Previewing

> ▶ **Reading Tip**

One way to preview is to **read the beginning sentence of each paragraph.** The first sentence often expresses the main idea of the paragraph. ▪

▷ Our names are an important part of our identity. This reading is about the traditions and practices of giving people names. Preview the reading. List three ideas you think you will learn from this reading.

1. _____
2. _____
3. _____

▷ Compare your ideas with a partner. Then, read the selection and check your predictions. Remove any ideas that you didn't find. Add any new ideas you found.

The Roots of Our Names

❶   Our first names are very familiar and important to us. Someone once estimated that we answer to our name 328,725 times during our lives. For most of us, our first name is given to us by our parents. There are many reasons why people choose to give certain names to their children. One of the most common practices is to name the child after a relative, or after one's self. Other reasons are more individual, like giving a name that has a pleasant sound or a positive association: for example, the name of a flower (Rose, Lily) or a quality (Faith, Joy, Hope). Some names come from famous people in history, like Joan after Joan of Arc or Winston after Winston Churchill. Other names come from famous entertainment personalities, like Elvis after Elvis Presley. Some people give their children names that are popular on television, like Ashley, Holly, or Kelly for girls and Brent, Keith, or Harrison for boys. Some people decide their children's names quickly; others think about the choices for much longer. Many parents think it's very important to find the right name for their child. Sometimes parents buy special baby-naming books and do other research, such as Internet searches, to find an appropriate name for their child.

❷   Our names can affect our personal lives. Some studies have found that children with the most popular first names are more favored by others. Some studies in England showed that, on average, children with common names like Mary and David received better grades from their teachers. Some studies show that the popularity of boys' names change less over time than girls' names. For example, since the 1950s the boy's name Michael has been in the top five most popular names. For girls, however, the popular names keep changing. Perhaps it's the feeling that tradition is more important for boys and beauty and style are more important for girls. In all languages there are names that are traditionally given to girls and others that are given to boys. But in English there are some names, such as Leslie and Robin, that can be used for either sex. In many languages there is a female and male version of the same name, such as Robert for a boy and Roberta for a girl. In many countries people give children a nickname that is often a short form of their first name, like Kate for Kathryn or Mike for Michael. Sometimes our names or nicknames can cause problems. Children who have a name commonly given to the opposite sex, who have an unpopular, old-fashioned, or strange-sounding name or an unusual nickname might be teased or made fun of by others. A boy named "Sue" or a girl named "John" will have problems as a result. Sometimes people decide to change their name. They select a new name to make their lives easier or to be more successful in their careers. Actors and performers such as Kirk Douglas and Madonna use stage names. Writers use pen names, or pseudonyms, when they publish their work. The writer Samuel Clemens is better known as Mark Twain and the English novelist George Eliot was actually a woman named Mary Ann Evans.

3 Family names also reflect different traditions. In China, people use their family name first and their given name second. In many Spanish-speaking countries, children take the family name of both parents. In Denmark, there are 85,000 different family names, but two-thirds of the population use only fifty of those for their last name. This creates problems for the government. It has trouble keeping files for so many people with the same first and last names. Over the last four hundred years, the Danish government has tried to get people to use different family names but with little success. Some family name changes do occur. When people emigrate to another country, they might alter or shorten their family name to fit in better with the general population. In the United States, when couples marry, some women decide to take their husband's family name, while others decide to keep their own name. The Indian province of Kerala is a matrilineal culture, where property is passed down from mother to daughter. Men who marry there adopt their wife's family name.

Getting the Main Idea

▶ Read the list of main ideas. Write the main idea for each of the paragraphs on the correct line.

Main Ideas

The traditions of family names in different countries.

Some traditions in choosing first names.

The effects that names have on people's lives.

Paragraph 1. _____

Paragraph 2. _____

Paragraph 3. _____

Scanning

 Reading Tip

Finding the main ideas helps you to **scan** for the answers to questions more effectively. When you read one of the questions below, ask yourself, "Which paragraph has the information I need to answer this question?" Then scan that paragraph first. ■

▶ **Getting the Facts** Answer the following questions. Underline the words in the reading that support your answer.

1. What are some of the traditions for choosing a first name?

   a. _____

   b. _____

   c. _____

2. a. What can happen to children who have a popular name?

   _____

   b. What can happen to children who have an unpopular name?

   _____

3. Why do some people change their names?

a. _____

b. _____

4. What are the traditions about family names in

China: _____

Spanish-speaking countries: _____

Denmark: _____

The United States: _____

Kerala, India: _____

▶ Compare answers with a partner. Refer to the reading if you have different answers.

Evaluating the Information

▶ **A Giving Your Opinion** Think about the following question: Should countries have rules and regulations about the names people can and cannot choose? If yes, what should these rules be? If no, why not?

▶ **B** Read the following paragraph. Find and underline facts that show names that are not allowed in different countries.

▶ **C** Work with a partner to compare the information you underlined. Check to see that you underlined the same information. Discuss your opinions on question A.

New Names: Who Decides?

Some countries have rules and regulations about the names people can and cannot choose. In France, officials can refuse to register a child's name if they think it is silly, insulting, or vulgar. In Quebec, Canada, there are also rules to follow in choosing a name. One Quebec couple had to fight to keep the name, Tomás, they wanted to give their son. The name was refused because it is written with an accent over the letter *a*. Officials said the accented *a* would make the name difficult for most people to pronounce. But, when the parents insisted that this name reflected their cultural heritage, the officials changed their decision. Another country that has name regulations is Norway. In Norway, a man who wanted to change his name to Harley Davidson, after his motorcycle, was refused. Officials said that Davidson was not a Norwegian name. Another rule is that Norwegians cannot choose a name that might be a social disadvantage for their child. Using the name of a cartoon character or a dictator is not allowed. On the other hand, in some countries, such as the United States and England, people may choose any name they wish. In these countries, people can easily change their name by going to court. For a small amount of money, they can legally register their new name.

▶ **D** Think about these questions. Share your ideas with others in a small group. Choose a group member to make a report of the ideas your group discusses and decides on.

a. What are some reasons why a country would refuse to allow a name?

b. What are the advantages (good points) of having rules for names?

c. What are the disadvantages (negative points)?

d. Do you think it is better to have rules for names or to allow people to choose any name they want?

▶Vocabulary Building

Word Form and Meaning

▶ **A** Match the words in Column A with their meanings in Column B.

Column A	Column B
_____ 1. alter	a. to control or manage something
_____ 2. appropriate	b. to list or record someone or something
_____ 3. register	c. to take something or make it your own
_____ 4. regulate	d. to choose someone or something
_____ 5. select	e. to change someone or something

▶ **B** Study these five words and their forms: verb, noun, adjective, and adverb. Then choose the correct form for each part of speech in the chart below. These words are commonly found in general and academic texts.

alter (v.)	appropriate (v.)	register (v.)	regulate (v.)	select (v.)
alteration (n.)	appropriation	registration	regulation	selective
alterability (n.)	appropriate	registered	regulator	selectively
altered (adj.)	appropriately	registry	regulatory	selection
alterable (adj.)		registrant	regulating	select
alterably (adv.)				selector

Verb	Noun	Adjective	Adverb
appropriate	1.	1.	1.
register	1.	1.	
	2.		
	3.		
regulate	1.	1.	
	2.	2.	
select	1.	1.	1.
	2.	2.	

▶ Compare lists with a partner. Try to agree on the same answers.

▶ **C** Write three or more sentences using words from the list.

▶ **D** In English, the form of a word can change when it is used as a different part of speech. In these sentences you will decide if you need a *noun* (an idea or a thing) or an *adjective* (a word that describes an idea or a thing). Choose the correct word to complete the sentences.

1. insult / insulting

   a. She didn't know that the words she used were an _____.

   b. She didn't mean to speak in an _____ way.

2. change / changing

   a. The student requested a _____ in his schedule.

   b. In these _____ times, new solutions are needed.

3. reflection / reflecting

   a. Her name was a _____ of her parents' hopes for the future.

   b. The _____ waters were calm and smooth.

4. try / trying

   a. She won the prize on her fifth _____ .

   b. People say that these are _____ times.

5. decision / deciding

   a. She cast the _____ vote in the election.

   b. She had to make a _____ quickly because time was running out.

▶ Compare answers with a partner.

▶ **E Synonyms** Circle the word that is closest in meaning to the word in boldface.

1. **allow**   leave   lift   let   lower

2. **choose**   select   suspend   separate   supply

3. **change**   advance   advise   alter   advantage

4. **create**   move   motivate   motion   make

5. **decide**   chance   choose   change   close

6. **receive**   give   get   go   grow

7. **refuse**   return   reject   reflect   remain

8. **register**   record   reason   repeat   read

▶ Write three or more sentences using words from the list.

Vocabulary in Context

▶ Complete each sentence with one of the following words from the reading. Circle the words in the sentence that helped you decide on your answer.

a. famous   b. individual   c. pleasant   d. popular
e. silly   f. successful   g. unusual

1. She chose a very _____ name that everyone liked.

2. They named their first child Elvis, after the _____ rock 'n' roll singer.

3. She decided to choose a name that had a _____ sound that was easy to pronounce.

4. He bought the picture because it had an _____ look that he had never seen before.

5. It was an _____ choice that only he could make.

6. She changed her name to be more _____ in her career.

7. She was afraid that her name would sound _____ to other people.

▶ Check your answers. Work with a partner and take turns reading the completed sentences.

Expanding Your Language

Reading

This reading explores a new twist on the idea of names. Notice how much easier it is to understand this text now that you have done some reading on the topic.

▶ First, read the following questions. After reading, answer them based on the information in the text.

1. How does Coca-Cola make sure that no other company copies its brand name?

2. How common is it to register a brand name?

3. a. What kind of names are common in the automotive industry?

   b. Why are these names popular?

4. a. What is one example of a product that needed a name for the international market?

   b. What does this example show?

5. Why would a corporation go to a company that specializes in finding new brand names?

The Business of Names

The right name is important in the business world. All you have to do is think of the names for some of the products you buy every day and you'll agree that the name and the product are linked in everyone's mind. Think of Coca-Cola. And its trade name Coke. In many countries, successful trade or brand names are protected by law. This is so that other companies cannot make a product that looks like another. People might think they were buying one product and, in fact, be buying something different. Businesses register a company or a product name with the government. In fact, it's estimated that more than 1,000 product and company names are registered every hour. Many companies spend a lot of money to find the right name for their products. A good example of this is in the automotive industry. Some of the most memorable and successful names for cars have powerful associations. The Ford Mustang, the Chevrolet Impala, and the Jaguar are only some examples of this trend of choosing the names of animals that are swift and strong. Harley-Davidson, the motorcycle company, has had its product become so famous that it registered the sound of its engine as well as its name.

When a U.S. company decides to sell its product in another country it has to make sure that the product name translates properly. When Coca-Cola introduced its soft drink to China, it looked for the right name. It wanted a name that would do two things. One was to project its image in Chinese and the second was to be close to its original brand name. It took several attempts before finding the right word—which sounds similar and translates as "happiness in the mouth." Asian company names are not new to the United States. The brand names of Samsung and Sony have been successful. Finding the right brand name is a big business. Asian companies that sell to foreign markets hire brand consultants to help find a name that will connect with its customers. There are even naming companies that specialize in inventing product names. These companies can charge up to $100,000 a word for their creations. But it's worth it. Successful companies know that the right association between a brand name and a product is important to its reputation and to its profitability.

Speaking

▶ **Oral Presentation** What are some customs for choosing names in your family or in your culture? Pepare information for a short (two-minute) talk on this subject. To help you get started, ask others in your class what they would like to know about the customs of choosing names. Think about the content of your talk. Try to give a few interesting details for each idea you explain. Put your ideas in order. Write your ideas in note form. Practice once or twice so that you are comfortable explaining the information to others. Present your information to a partner or in a small group.

Writing

▶ **Topic Writing** From the ideas you have gathered in this chapter and your own experience, write about some customs of choosing names that are important or interesting to you. Follow the instructions for "Topic Writing" in Chapter 1, pages 12 and 13.

▶ **Opinion Writing** Write about whether or not countries should make rules about the names people can choose for themselves or their children. Use information from the reading to support your ideas. Include any ideas or examples of your own.

 *Online Study Center*   For additional activities, go to the *Reading Matters* Online Study Center at *college.hmco.com/pic/wholeytwo2e.*

5 Researching Our Hidden Roots

Chapter Openers

Listing Ideas

◉ What special or surprising events could lead you to look into your family history? Give some reasons that people could have for finding out about their family history.

1. inheriting money from an unknown relative

2. _____

3. _____

4. _____

◉ Share your ideas with a partner or with a small group.

Categorizing

◉ Check (✔) the category you think best fits each of these feelings.

Feelings	Positive	Negative	Neutral (Either/Both)
lonely			
stunned			
amazed			
excited			
nervous			
embarrassed			
uncomfortable			
angry			
thrilled			
surprised			
overjoyed			
curious			
upset			

▶ Compare answers with a partner. Choose several of these feelings and talk about times when you felt that way.

❯Paired Readings

▶ Choose one of the readings. Work with a partner who is reading the same story.

❶John's Story

Skimming

▶ Read this selection quickly and answer the following question:

What surprising information did John find out?

_____

A Surprising Discovery

❶   John O'Neill was an only child who lived with his parents in Albany, New York. The O'Neills had a lot of friends but not many relatives. John knew his mother had a half sister who lived in California, but John had never met her. John's mother didn't have much contact with her sister. John's father was an only child, just like his son. When John was twenty years old, his parents died in a car accident and John was left alone in the large house where he had grown up. John felt lonely and uncomfortable living in his childhood home, so he decided to sell the house. Once the stress of selling the house was over, he had to look through all the papers and the belongings of his parents and decide what memorabilia he wanted to keep to remember them by and what to throw away.

2   One afternoon John found a large, thick envelope filled with official-looking papers and some twenty-year-old newspaper clippings. He started to read and was amazed by what he learned. According to the papers, he had been adopted by his parents when he was an infant. Even more curious was the fact that another child, a girl, had been born at the same time. He had a twin sister somewhere! John was stunned. He felt angry that his parents hadn't told him about his background but thrilled to think that he might have family he had not known about. Now he had to try to find the sister he had no memories of. He had to learn the identity of his birth parents. He wondered where his investigation would take him. He went on the Internet and entered the words "looking for birth parents" into a search engine. He found ways he could look for his birth parents. He also learned that it could take up to two years to get any useful information at all. He prepared himself for a long search that might not be successful. To begin with, he had the name of the hospital where he and his sister were born, the adoption papers his parents signed, and the date of their birth. He decided to begin pursuing his search there.

Understanding Details

▷ **Information Questions** Look for the answers to these questions. Underline the words in the story that support your answer.

1. What was the size of John's family?

    _____

2. What did John find after his parents died?

    _____

3. What two things did John find out about his background?

    a. _____

    b. _____

4. a. What did John decide to do?

    _____

    b. Where did he go to find information?

    _____

    c. What did he learn?

    _____

　　d. What did he prepare himself for?

　　_____

　　e. What information did he have to begin his search?

　　_____

▶ Work with a partner. Try to agree on the same answers. Refer to the reading in cases where you disagree.

Note Taking

▶ List the facts of the story in note form on pages of your own.

John's story
• an only child
•
•
•

Recapping the Story

▶ Work with a partner who took notes on the same story.

▶ 1. Orally, compare the list of facts you wrote.
   2. Check that the facts you wrote are clear and understandable.
   3. Refer to the reading if you have different information.
   4. Change or add to the facts you noted as necessary.
   5. Taking turns, practice reporting the information.

Reacting to the Story

▶ Share your ideas about these questions with a partner.

1. If you were John, how would you feel?
2. What questions would John want to ask his sister?
3. How do you think this story could end?

②Joy's Story

Skimming   ▶ Read this selection quickly and answer the following question:

What surprising information did Joy find out?

_____

What's Your Medical History?

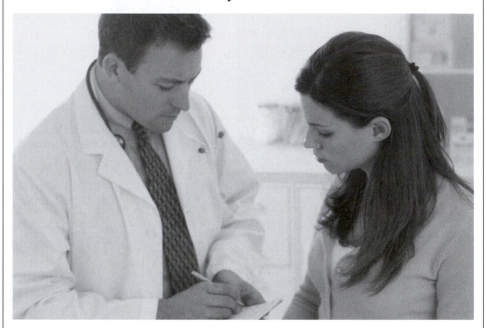

①   Joy Kaplan was newly married and had just moved from Chicago to San Francisco with her husband. Soon after moving, she found that she was pregnant. She was overjoyed at the idea of having a baby but a little worried about being far from her family, her friends, and all the support she had back home. She asked several people for recommendations, chose a doctor near her home, and made an initial appointment. Because she was a new patient, the doctor asked her a lot of questions about her family. He asked about the ages and medical history of her brothers and sisters, her parents, her aunts and uncles, and even her grandparents. Joy was surprised to find that she didn't have a lot of answers for the doctor. She felt uncomfortable and embarrassed about the amount of information she didn't have. Why did the doctor need data such as her grandparents' medical history? The doctor understood her feelings and wasn't surprised at her reaction.

❷   The doctor knew Joy was upset, so he explained that he had important, life-saving reasons for finding out about the medical histories of her relatives. This information could help her have a healthy pregnancy. If there was a family history of diabetes or heart disease, the doctor would watch for signs of these problems during Joy's pregnancy. Also, he could help identify medical problems the unborn baby might have and, if possible, prevent or prepare to treat them. The doctor needed to know if there had been any genetically-transmitted diseases in her or her husband's family. He wanted to know if her mother had had problems such as miscarriages or premature births in her pregnancies. He also wanted to know if there was a family history of multiple births, such as twins or triplets. Joy thought she remembered that one of her grandmothers had a twin brother or sister, and she was curious. Did this mean that there was a greater chance that she could have twins? Were there any hidden medical problems she didn't know about? Where should she begin to look? The doctor suggested she start her medical history by asking her parents for information about as many of her relatives as possible. Joy was excited but a little nervous about what she might discover. She called a friend back home who reassured her that her feelings were normal and that she had had the same experience. Her friend gave her two good suggestions. She could begin by constructing a family tree with all the medical information she could gather. She could also check by going online and searching for more information about the types of procedures, like ultrasounds, that doctors use to check on the health of an unborn baby. Joy felt better after talking to her friend and she decided to begin by phoning her parents and her parents-in-law to begin her search that evening.

Understanding Details

▶ **Information Questions** Look for the answers to these questions. Underline the words in the story that support your answer.

1. Why did Joy move to a new city?

_____

2. How did Joy feel about her pregnancy?

_____

3. a. What questions did the doctor ask her?

   _____

   b. How did she feel about the doctor's questions?

   _____

4. What two reasons did the doctor give Joy for the questions he asked?

   a. _____

   b. _____

5. What are some examples of medical conditions the doctor wanted to know about?

   a. _____

   b. _____

   c. _____

6. What did Joy's friend suggest she do?

   a. _____

   b. _____

7. What did Joy decide to do?

   _____

🔘 Work with a partner. Try to agree on the answers. Refer to the reading in cases where you disagree.

Note Taking

🔘 List the facts of the story in note form on pages of your own.

Joy's story
• newly married
•
•
•

Recapping the Story

🔘 Work with a partner who took notes about the same story. Follow the instructions for recapping on page 57.

Reacting to the Story

▶ Share your ideas about these questions with a partner.

1. If you were Joy, how would you feel?
2. What questions do you think Joy should ask her family?
3. How do you think this story could end?

Retelling the Story

▶ Work with a partner who took notes about the other story. Use your notes to retell the information.

Comparing the Readings

Discussing the Stories

▶ Answer these questions based on the information from the stories.

1. What is each person's motivation for finding out about his or her past?
2. What are the similarities and differences in the two stories?
3. What do you think could be the conclusion of these stories? What do you think John and Joy will find out? How could they discover this information?

Vocabulary Building

Word Form and Meaning

▶ **A** Match the words in Column A with their meanings in Column B.

Column A	Column B
_____ 1. investigate	a. to suggest or approve something to another
_____ 2. pursue	b. to cause worry or pressure
_____ 3. transmit	c. to look into, study or explore
_____ 4. recommend	d. to go after, chase or follow up on something or someone
_____ 5. stress	e. to give

▶ **B** Study these five words and their forms: verb, noun, adjective, and adverb. Then choose the correct form for each part of speech in the chart below. These words are commonly found in general and academic texts.

investigate (v.)   pursue (v.)   recommend (v.)   stress (v.)   transmit (v.)
investigation (n.)   pursuit   recommendation   stress   transmission
investigator (n.)   pursued   recommended   stressed   transmitter
investigatory (adj.)   pursuing   recommending   stressful   transmitted
investigating (adj.)   pursuer   stressfully   transmittal
                                                                 stressor

Verb	Noun	Adjective	Adverb
pursue	1. 2.	1. 2.	
recommend	1.	1. 2.	
stress	1. 2.	1. 2.	1.
transmit	1. 2. 3.	1.	

▶ Compare lists with a partner. Try to agree on the same answers.

▶ **C** Write three or more sentences using words from the list.

▶ **D** Choose the correct word to complete the sentences. Use your knowledge of grammar rules (i.e., if the word is a noun, adjective, verb, or adverb) to help you choose.

1. pregnant / pregnancy

   a. She was very happy when she found out about her _____.

   b. She told the doctor that she thought she was _____.

2. genetic / genetically

   a. She was worried that she could have inherited a _____ disease.

   b. She was worried that the disease could be transmitted _____.

3. question / questioned

   a. She decided she would ask her doctor the _____ that was on her mind.

   b. She wondered about the doctor's decision and _____ him about it.

4. memories / remember / memorabilia

   a. He looked through all the boxes to see what _____ he wanted to keep.

   b. She tried to _____ her grandmother's medical history.

   c. She had a lot of _____ of her grandmother, but nothing was written down.

▶ **E Verbs: Present and Past** Write the past form of the following verbs. Circle these past tense verbs in the reading.

1. adopt _____   6. amaze _____

2. choose _____   7. explain _____

3. fill _____   8. find _____

4. learn _____   9. need _____

5. suggest _____   10. wonder _____

▶ Check your answers. Write three or more sentences and three or more questions of your own, using both the present and past forms of any of these verbs.

Vocabulary in Context

▶ Use your understanding of one part of the sentence to help you guess the verb/preposition combination that is missing. Remember that sometimes when a verb is followed by a preposition, it has a special meaning. Complete each sentence with one of the following phrases.

a. adopted by   b. grown up   c. known about   d. look through
e. throw away   f. watch for   g. worried about

1. He decided to _____ all the papers he found to try to locate the name he needed.

2. He didn't know that he had been _____ his parents when he was a baby.

3. She wondered why she hadn't _____ her mother's first marriage.

4. She had _____ in a small family and liked to visit them often.

5. She had too many papers to keep, so she decided to _____ half of them.

6. Joy didn't want to be _____ the pregnancy, but she was.

7. He told her what signs of trouble she should _____.

▶ Check your answers. Work with a partner and take turns reading your sentences.

Expanding Your Language

Reading This reading explores a true story on the topic of finding your roots. Notice how much easier it is to understand this text now that you have done some reading on the topic.

▶ First, read the following questions. After reading, answer them based on the information in the text.

1. Who were James Raymond's adoptive parents?
2. Where did James grow up?
3. What interest did James have?
4. Why did James look for his birth parents?
5. What did he discover?
6. How did he react to learning the identity of his birth father?
7. Why did James decide to see his father?
8. What happened after the two men decided to meet?
9. How has James's relationship to his birth father and his adoptive family changed?

Destiny: A Father and Child Reunion

The expression "following in his father's footsteps" could certainly fit James Raymond. But it didn't appear that obvious at the start. James Raymond grew up in Southern California as the adopted son of Madeline and John Raymond. As a boy, James sang in the church choir and started to learn the piano. He had a natural talent for music and studied music in college, graduating from California State University. Then, he started out on his musical career. As a keyboardist, he toured with jazz artists and even worked with the Spice Girls. He worked in television recording as well.

As he was planning to marry, his adoptive parents suggested that it would be a good time for him to learn about his birth parents. James agreed and began his search. A few months later he got a call saying that his birth mother was looking for him. She lived in Australia and worked on an arts council there. The two met just before Raymond's wedding. His birth mother then told James the news that would change his life. His biological father was a famous rock musician, David Crosby from the legendary 60s rock and roll band "Crosby, Stills and Nash."

At first James Raymond thought that it was another David Crosby. He didn't have any of his famous father's music, so he went out to listen to as much of it as he could. At first, he didn't want to contact Crosby. He felt he needed time to think about it all. He was happy in his own life and didn't want Crosby to think he wanted anything from him. Then, a year later, Raymond heard that Crosby was seriously ill with liver disease and might die. He decided that it was time for him to meet his biological father. Crosby was delighted to hear from him. He had

wondered all these years about the boy he had given up for adoption.

Now the father and son are making music together. Crosby and Raymond are performing on stage together with guitarist Jeff Pevar in a three person band called CPR. David Crosby is proud of Raymond's musical talents. He feels happy to know that his son grew into such a fine musician and a good man. Does David Crosby wish he had kept his son? Truthfully, he feels that Raymond would not have had an easy time growing up with him as a father. Remembering his past life, Crosby knows he wouldn't have been a good parent. How does Raymond feel? Sometimes, when he is on stage with his father, Raymond feels as though it is a dream. Then, he thinks that he is where he belongs. Raymond's adoptive father, John Raymond, says he feels blessed. "We didn't lose a son, we gained a new family."

Speaking

▶ **Role Play** Work with a partner. Choose one of the stories in this chapter to act out. Write out a conversation based on the ideas in the story. You may want to add characters (such as a friend for John to talk to or Joy's husband) to the story. Here is one example of how to begin the conversation:

John: Can you meet me at the cafe? The most amazing thing just happened. I have to talk to you.
Friend: Sure. I can be at the cafe in ten minutes.

▶ Use your lines to act out the story, but do not memorize the lines. Be creative.

Writing

▶ **Reacting to a Story** Use your notes to write about one of the stories in this chapter. Write your own reaction to the story. What do you think the person should do?

 *Online Study Center* For additional activities, go to the *Reading Matters* Online Study Center at *college.hmco.com/pic/wholeytwo2e.*

6 Writing Our Own History

Chapter Openers

Personalizing

> Reading Tip

Thinking about **your own ideas and experiences** on a topic is called personalizing. This helps you to recognize language in the reading and will help you understand more easily. ■

▷ Imagine that your grandmother gave you a scrapbook about her life. What do you think the scrapbook would contain? List as many ideas as you can.

1. *her wedding invitation*

2. _____

3. _____

4. _____

Checklist

▷ Check the ways that you record important events in your life or in the life of your family.

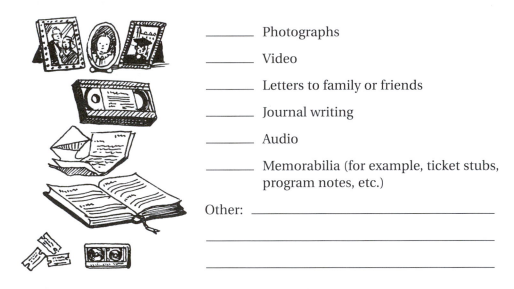

_____ Photographs

_____ Video

_____ Letters to family or friends

_____ Journal writing

_____ Audio

_____ Memorabilia (for example, ticket stubs, program notes, etc.)

Other: _____

_____

▷ Work with a partner. Choose two important events in your life. Describe what you remember about what happened. Tell how you recorded these events.

Exploring and Understanding Reading

Previewing

This reading explains one woman's ideas on the importance of writing autobiographies. Look at the title and subtitle. What do you predict the reading will be about?

1. _____
2. _____
3. _____

Skimming

> Reading Tip

Skimming is a useful strategy when you have a **longer reading with difficult or unfamiliar vocabulary.** When you skim, you skip over the words you don't know and focus on what you can understand. Read for the idea. ▪

Skim the reading and see if your predictions were correct. If you think you were wrong, change your prediction. After your quick reading, answer these general questions.

1. What does Marie Bolton think is important to do?

_____

2. Why does she think it's important?

_____

Our Own Stories

Autobiographical writing helps us record memories, feel connected

By Ann Douglas

Peterborough, Ont.—One of Marie Bolton's greatest treasures is a scrapbook that was lovingly compiled for her by her grandmother. It's filled with photographs, postcards, poems, Christmas cards, and other memorabilia accumulated over the course of ninety-four years.

Bolton sees the scrapbook as a precious legacy from her grandmother, who is no longer living.

"When I read the scrapbook, I learn things about my grandmother that I wouldn't otherwise have known," Bolton explained. "I discover her feelings about the grandfather I never knew. I hear her recall the joy and wonder of caring for her babies when they were young, and I witness world events like the end of World War I as seen through her eyes."

Bolton, 33, a freelance writer in Peterborough, was so moved by the scrapbook that she began leading workshops on the art of memoir writing.

"It's my way of encouraging others, particularly older people, to write about their lives. Many people are reluctant to write about themselves because they feel that their life has been terribly ordinary and is not likely to be of interest to anyone else.

"I believe that we all have a story to tell, and that we owe it to others to share our experience."

Autobiographical writing doesn't have to be that difficult, Bolton said.

"It's important to give yourself permission to start and stop the project as your time and interest permit," she said.

"Sometimes it's necessary to put the project aside for a few weeks or even months if things get particularly busy at home or at work."

Bolton said the hardest part of autobiographical writing is getting started. "If you're lucky enough to have a closet full of shoeboxes filled with treasures that date back years and years, flip through these boxes and start to think about how the various pieces fit into the major periods in your life, i.e., childhood, school days, career, marriage, childbearing, retirement, etc.

"Then purchase a scrapbook and start piecing your materials together chronologically. Select photos, artwork, report cards, ticket stubs, wedding invitations, and other memorabilia that are significant to you, and then record the memories that they trigger for you."

Judy Brenna, 55, took this type of approach when she sat down to record her family memories.

"Last Christmas, I put together a binder of all my family's recipes for my four children. With each recipe, I included a paragraph about how I came by the recipe and whose recipe it was.

"It turned into a trip down memory lane, remembering when I was a child helping my mother to duplicate her mother's favorite family dishes or when I was a young bride trying to re-create my husband's mother's perfect recipe.

"I ended up creating something of a family history of happy times spent in the kitchen and around the dining room table."

While creating a scrapbook can be time-consuming, it may be one of the most important projects you'll ever undertake, Bolton said.

"My grandmother has been dead for two years now," she said. "While I can no longer chat with her over a cup of tea about days gone by, I can flip through the scrapbook and reflect on her memories of yesteryear.

"It helps me to remember her and to get an appreciation of what it's like to live a long and happy life. That's her legacy to me."

Checking the Facts

▷ **A** Circle *T* for true and *F* for false. Underline the information in the reading that supports your answer. Correct any information that is false.

1. T F   Marie Bolton's grandmother is still living.

2. T F   Marie decided to teach others to write memoirs.

3. T F   People feel that their lives are interesting to many others.

4. T F   The easiest part of writing an autobiography is getting started.

5. T F   Marie likes to look through her grandmother's scrapbook.

▶ **B** Search the reading to answer the following questions.

1. What are three things that Marie learned about her grandmother?

   a. _____

   b. _____

   c. _____

2. What work does Marie Bolton do?

   _____

3. What are six major periods of a person's life?

   a. _____   d. _____

   b. _____   e. _____

   c. _____   f. _____

4. What are the steps for creating a scrapbook?

   a. Start collecting and organizing memorabilia.

   b. Purchase _____

   c. Start _____

   d. Select _____

   e. Record _____

5. What are two reasons why Marie feels creating a scrapbook is important?

   a. _____

   b. _____

▶ Work with a partner. Take turns reading the questions and answers orally. Refer to the reading in cases where you disagree.

Relating Main Ideas and Details

▶ Reread the story quickly and underline the details for each of the following main ideas. Write the letter of each main idea in the margin where you found the details.

A. The gift Marie Bolton got

B. The work Marie Bolton does

C. The steps to creating a scrapbook

D. The importance of Marie Bolton's work

▶ With a partner, take turns explaining the details of these ideas in your own words.

Giving Your Opinion

▶ Decide if you agree or disagree with these statements taken from the reading. Be prepared to explain the reasons for your opinions.

1. Many people feel that their life has been terribly ordinary and is not likely to be of interest to anyone else.
2. I believe that we all have a story to tell, and that we owe it to others to share our experience.

▶ Share your ideas with a partner or with a small group. Together find another statement from the reading that you think is interesting or important. Discuss the reasons for your choice.

Applying the Information

▶ **Discovering the Reasons People Write** In the first reading Marie Bolton lists some reasons people write about their own lives. These reasons include the following:

A. Recording our thoughts and feelings about things that happened
B. Witnessing world events in a personal way
C. Feeling connected to others
D. Finding out about important life events
E. Recording memories for the future

▶ The following is a short autobiographical story. Read the story and, as you read, think about the list of reasons from the first reading in the chapter. What do you think the author's reason is for writing? Circle the reason(s) in the list above.

My Life as a Sandwich

By Dr. Barbara Roback

❶   There were three of them, aged 87, 89, and 91, all sisters of my mother. They are in varying states of decline now—one in a retirement home, one in a chronic care facility, and the eldest one still living alone, despite the lack of vision, hearing, balance, and judgment. She, of course, insists that she's fine and continues to smoke, fall, and give money away to the drugstore delivery man. He is doing nicely, thank you, with his secondhand stretch limo, thanks to quite a few of those "loans." Meanwhile, various agency workers and one niece tear out their increasingly gray hair. She has recently started having hallucinations about Greek and Roman statues. "Is that frightening?" I ask. "No, I saw statues as a child when I was in Europe," she says matter-of-factly.

2   On the other jaw of the vise grip are my six-year-old boys, fraternal twins, who need endless cuddling, stories, baths, lunches, rides to lessons, nagging, and refereeing. They don't understand why they have to visit smelly institutions where old people scream and try to hug them. Nor do they understand why their mother yells at her 91-year-old aunt for giving thousands of dollars away. Such is the life of my generation, sandwiched as we are between caring for aging relatives and young children. Most of us, out of desire and necessity, also work outside the home. Where is the time or energy for keeping the marriage fires burning?

3   But there are significant rewards that come from life in a vise. This summer I packed up one aunt's abandoned apartment. She had been an invalid most of her life; teenage tuberculosis had robbed her of her strength and mobility. Because I lost both my parents at a young age, she became guardian to me and my older sister, doing the best she could to care for both of us. As a teenager I was embarrassed by my abnormal family and retreated into writing stories about imaginary characters who led truly wonderful lives. But this summer, as I sifted through the remains of years of accumulation, I found some amazing treasures: my mother's high school ring from 1936, my sister's hospital birth tag, a desperate letter written by my mother, overwhelmed with the responsibility of caring for her dying husband and her two too-young daughters. And then, the ceremonial wine from my parents' wedding, lovingly kept from 1939. My years of shame and resentment evaporated. I was now back to myself.

4   My aunt was a superb seamstress and her fabrics, sewing machine, and threads have been donated to help equip a Training Center for immigrant women to become employable. My aunt is settled in her new hospital home. I beg and bribe my children into visiting her with promises of treats. They walk down the hallway holding their noses. But in the end, they do kiss her good-bye. And I pray they are learning something important about human decency.

❯Vocabulary Building

Word Form and Meaning

▷ **A** Match the words in Column A with their meanings in Column B.

Column A

_____ 1. abandon

_____ 2. accumulate

_____ 3. appreciate

_____ 4. permit

_____ 5. photograph

Column B

a. to gather or collect

b. to be aware of the importance of or to value someone or something

c. to allow something or let someone do something

d. to take a picture of someone or something

e. to leave or let go of someone or something

▷ **B** Study these five words and their forms: verb, noun, adjective, and adverb. Then choose the correct form for each part of speech in the chart below. These words are commonly found in general and academic texts.

abandon (v.)	accumulate (v.)	appreciate (v.)	permit (v.)	photograph (v.)
abandonment (n.)	accumulation	appreciation	permitted	photograph
abandon (n.)	accumulator	appreciative	permission	photographer
abandoned (adj.)	accumulating	appreciatively	permit	photographically
	accumulated	appreciated	permissive	photographed
				photographic

Verb	Noun	Adjective	Adverb
accumulate	1.	1.	
	2.	2.	
appreciate	1.	1.	1.
		2.	
permit	1.	1.	
	2.	2.	
photograph	1.	1.	1.
	2.	2.	

▷ Compare lists with a partner. Try to agree on the same answers.

▶ **C** Write three or more sentences using words from the list.

▶ **D Roots** Words that come from the same root, like these words from the Latin *memorabilis*, have similar meanings. Choose the correct word to complete the sentence.

memoir / remember / memorabilia / memories

1. I have a lot of very warm _____ of growing up in my grandmother's house.

2. I gathered all the _____ my mother had collected and put them into a big box.

3. I tried to create a book that would help people _____ this special time in their lives.

4. She decided to begin to write a _____ of her own life.

▶ **E Matching Meanings** Match the phrases in Column A to those closest in meaning in Column B.

Column A	Column B
_____ 1. end up	a. look at something quickly
_____ 2. put together	b. have strong feelings
_____ 3. flip through	c. talk about everyday events
_____ 4. chat with	d. have a final product
_____ 5. be moved by	e. create something from different parts
_____ 6. reflect on	f. think about the meaning of things

Vocabulary in Context

▶ You can understand the meaning of a new word by using the words you know to help you make a good guess. Circle the words that help you to guess the meaning of words in boldface.

1. In this unit you will read about one of the fastest-growing interests in North America—**genealogy**. Looking into our family history is the third most popular hobby in the United States.

2. It's filled with different items from the past, like photographs, postcards, poems, Christmas cards, and other **memorabilia** accumulated over the course of ninety-four years.

3. I **witness** events like the end of World War I as seen through her eyes.

4. Many people are **reluctant** to write about themselves. They hesitate because they feel that their life has been terribly ordinary and is not likely to be of interest to anyone else.

5. Start to think about how the various pieces fit into the major periods of your life, i.e., childhood, school days, career, marriage, retirement, etc. Then, purchase a scrapbook and start piecing your materials together **chronologically**.

6. My grandmother has been dead for two years now. But the scrapbook she made helps me to remember her and to get an appreciation of what it's like to live a long and happy life. That's her **legacy** to me.

Expanding Your Language

Speaking

▷ **A Tell and Retell** Quickly reread the story "My Life as a Sandwich." Highlight the important details of the story. Get together with a partner. Take turns telling the information in each paragraph. Tell as much as you can remember.

▷ **B Two-Minute Taped Talk** Choose a person who is important to you. It can be a family member, a friend, or someone you admire. Prepare a two-minute audiotape or audio CD to talk about this person and the effect they have had on your life. Base your talk on your own ideas and the information in this chapter. Make a short outline of your ideas in note form. Practice your talk a few times before you record.

Writing

▷ **Topic Writing** Imagine that you are going to make a scrapbook about your life. Choose three items of memorabilia that you would include and write about what each one means to you. Follow the instructions in Chapter 1, pages 12 and 13.

Read On: Taking It Further

Reading Suggestions

Remember to **write in your reading journal** and add **vocabulary log entries** to your journal. ■

Ask your teacher to recommend some easy-to-read autobiographical or biographical titles for you to choose from. Reading these types of stories is a good way to find out about people and the times and places they lived in.

Sample Suggestion: In *Roots*, Alex Haley wrote about his family history, going back to when one of his ancestors was brought from Africa into the United States as a slave. Haley's family story is very interesting. You could find out about this story by looking for the video of the television program based on his book.

 *Online Study Center*   For additional activities, go to the *Reading Matters* Online Study Center at *college.hmco.com/pic/wholeytwo2e.*

UNIT 3

Money Matters

When money
talks, the world
keeps silent.

—*Swedish Proverb*

Introducing the Topic

Money affects our daily lives. It influences the way we feel, think, and act. This unit will look into some interesting questions about money. Chapter 7 will examine what young people can learn about the value of money. Is a person ever too young to start thinking about budgets and savings? Chapter 8 looks at the impact of lotteries on people's lives. Lotteries and other forms of gambling are popular in many countries. Are they a good thing? Chapter 9 is about the future of money. Will credit, debit, and other bank cards totally replace cash? How will this affect our attitudes toward money?

▶Points of Interest

Expressions

▶ Read and decide if you think each expression shows a positive, negative, or neutral attitude toward money. Check (✔) the category you decide on.

	Positive	Negative	Neutral
1. Love of money is the root of all evil.	_____	_____	_____
2. A penny saved is a penny earned.	_____	_____	_____
3. Time is money.	_____	_____	_____
4. Money can't buy love.	_____	_____	_____
5. Money doesn't grow on trees.	_____	_____	_____
6. Money speaks in a language all nations understand.	_____	_____	_____

▶ Work with a partner. Discuss what the expressions mean and try to agree on the best category for each.

7 Starting Young: Learning the Value of Money

Chapter Openers

Discussion Questions

▶ Think about these questions. Share your ideas with a partner or with a small group.

1. Have you ever made a budget or a savings plan for yourself?
2. What are some common problems that people have when they try to save and budget money?
3. a. Did you ever get an allowance (money from your parents)?
   b. What was it for?
4. How much allowance money should a child have at the following ages: 2–5, 6–11, 12–16, 16–18?
5. Who taught you the most about handling money?
   a. Mother
   b. Father
   c. Both mother and father
   d. Teacher
   e. Friend or other

Exploring and Understanding Reading

Predicting

▶ Circle *A* if you agree or *D* if you disagree with each statement.

1. A D   Children usually know how much money their parents make.
2. A D   It is a good idea to give children an allowance at age two.
3. A D   Children learn about money from their parents' example.
4. A D   At age seven, children can learn to shop for the best price.
5. A D   Children should start saving for college by age twelve.
6. A D   Teenagers should not work after school.

▶ Work with a partner. Compare your answers. You don't have to agree, but explain your reasons as completely as possible. After you finish reading, return to these questions and answer them based on the information you read.

Skimming

▶ Read the selection quickly and choose the statement that best expresses the general idea of the reading as a whole.

a. Parents should not talk about money with their children until they are older.

b. Parents should get experts to teach their children about money.

c. Parents should give their children different advice about money depending on their age.

Can We Teach Kids to Save?

❶   Money management experts think that children need to learn about money at an early age. They advise parents to give kids four years old or younger a weekly allowance. Experts suggest parents give preschool children two or three dollars a week and then add a dollar at every birthday. This might seem like a large amount of money for a child that young. However, experts say that if parents want their children to understand how to budget money, it's not. Even preschool children can learn the value of money.

❷   Young children don't always know how much money their parents make, or understand how their parent's earnings affect them. But parents can assist their children with developing some very important attitudes no matter what their incomes are. Kids can learn to tell the difference between what they want and what they need. They can learn how to make a budget and how to keep spending within that budget. For example, when children want an expensive toy that costs more than they have in allowance, parents can help them figure out how many weeks it will take to save the money to buy it. In the end, the most important way parents influence their children's attitudes toward money is by setting a good example of responsible money management in the way they budget, spend, and save money themselves.

❸   Here are some age-specific suggestions for teaching responsible attitudes toward money.

Ages 2–5

- Give a small allowance ($2–3) each week. It can be for doing chores (making their bed, cleaning their room, etc.) or not.
- Let children pay for some of the things they want, such as a toy or a special treat.

- Budget a certain amount of the money for savings.
- Discuss what they will use their savings for, i.e., school, travel, gifts, etc.

Ages 6–12

- Increase their allowance gradually to match their age ($6 or 7 for a six-year-old). Show children how to make a budget.
- Set up a savings account at the bank in the child's name.
- Talk about ways to earn extra money (contract for special chores and small jobs in the neighborhood such as shoveling snow or raking leaves).
- Show children how to be better consumers by shopping for the best price.

Ages 13–17

- Encourage children to earn more of their own money at small jobs after school.
- Give children responsibility for paying part of their school or extracurricular expenses such as sports equipment or musical instruments.
- Have children open a checking account and handle their own money.
- Have children save money for future schooling costs such as college tuition.

If kids start on the road to good money management when they are young, they will be learning an important life skill. They may make some mistakes along the way, but they will learn the basics of saving, investing, budgeting, and wise spending. Kids who learn about money early are often good at making money later. And that's good news for parents.

Understanding Details

◐ Circle the correct answer. Underline the words in the reading that support your answer.

1. Experts suggest that parents begin to give children an allowance at age _____.
   a. two or three
   b. six or seven
   c. eight or nine

2. Children often _____ how much money their parents earn.

   a. know   b. don't know

3. Children _____ learn the difference between what they want and what they need.

   a. can

   b. can't

4. Parents can influence their children's attitudes toward money the most by _____.

   a. telling them what to do

   b. setting a good example

5. Children can start to work after school at age _____.

   a. seven

   b. ten

   c. thirteen

6. It's good for kids to learn money management at a young age because they will _____.

   a. learn to spend wisely

   b. spend more money

   c. make more money later

▶ Compare answers with a partner. Look back at the reading if you disagree.

Reacting to the Story

▶ Share your ideas about these questions with a partner or a small group.

1. a. Is it possible for parents to teach their children positive attitudes toward money?

   b. How difficult or how easy is it? How important is it?

2. When do we learn our attitudes toward money? Can these attitudes change?

Applying the Information

▶ **Problem Solving** Based on the information you read, what would you suggest in the following situations?

1. Your seventeen-year-old wants to apply to a university that has a very high tuition.

Suggestions: _____

2. You are out shopping and your five-year-old asks you to buy an expensive toy that is being advertised on TV.

Suggestions: _____

3. Your fourteen-year-old wants to get a part-time job after school.

Suggestions: _____

4. Your eleven-year-old wants to do extra chores to earn more money.

Suggestions: _____

▶ Compare your suggestions. Make a list of the best suggestions and report them to the class.

Evaluating the Information

▶ Read the short article that follows and then discuss these questions.

1. What is this child doing?
2. What is this child and the children he advises learning?
3. What are the positive points of this boy's job? What information surprises you?
4. Should this child be working? Why or why not?

Should This Child Be Working?

Andrew Burns, all of nine years old, greets customers in his capacity as president of the Children's Bank at Enterprise Bank of Omaha. "I understand banking," says the fourth-grader, who dreamed up the job and then applied for it at his father's bank. "And I'm a kid. I know what their needs are." Among the kiddy bank's services are making loans of up to $100 to youngsters (with an adult cosigner) and enabling paper carriers and other kids with jobs to deposit money in zipper bags the way businesses do. There's also a teller window low enough for children to reach. Andrew comes in two or three times a week to serve his clientele. "If they're in trouble with money, if they need some advice, I help them," he says.

Evaluating Suggestions

▶ There are many approaches to the subject of money. These can differ from family to family and from country to country. From your own experience, give your opinion of some of the suggestions in the reading. Discuss one or more of these questions with a partner or a small group.

1. Should teenagers work to make money while still in school?
2. Should children know details of the family budget?
3. Should young people borrow money to complete their college education?

▶Vocabulary Building

Word Form and Meaning

▶ **A** Match the words in Column A with their meanings in Column B.

Column A

_____ 1. affect

_____ 2. contract

_____ 3. deposit

_____ 4. enable

_____ 5. specify

Column B

a. to determine or show something particular or special

b. to touch someone's feeling or to influence or change someone or something

c. to make it possible for someone to do something

d. to make a legal agreement with someone

e. to put something (e.g., money) somewhere

▶ **B** Study these five words and their forms: verb, noun, adjective, and adverb. Then choose the correct form for each part of speech in the chart below. These words are commonly found in general and academic texts.

affect (v.)	contract (v.)	deposit (v.)	enable (v.)	specify (v.)
affective (adj.)	contractor	depositing	enabling	specification
affected (adj.)	contracting	deposit	enabler	specific
affecting (adj.)	contract	depositor	enabled	specifically
	contracted	deposited		specified

Verb	Noun	Adjective	Adverb
contract	1.	1.	
	2.	2.	
deposit	1.	1.	
	2.	2.	
enable	1.	1.	
		2.	
specify	1.	1.	1.
		2.	

▶ Compare lists with a partner. Try to agree on the same answers.

▶ **C** Write three or more sentences using words from the list.

▶ **D** Many words have more than one meaning. Look at these definitions for the word *contract*.

a. **contract (noun):** a legal agreement between two or more people
b. **contract (verb):** to make an agreement
c. **contract (verb):** to shorten or shrink
d. **contract (adjective):** area of law having to do with agreements

▶ Read the sentences below and write the letter of the correct meaning on the line provided.

1. _____ She spent many years studying the details of **contract** law.

2. _____ She felt the material **contract** as it hit the cold air.

3. _____ The couple agreed to sign the marriage **contract**.

4. _____ She asked the building manager to **contract** for the necessary renovations to the apartment.

5. _____ She felt her muscles **contract** as she prepared to exercise.

Vocabulary in Context

▶ **A** Complete each sentence with one of the following phrases. Use your understanding of the general meaning of the sentence to help you.

a. tell the difference   b. make a budget   c. keep their spending
d. figure out   e. setting a good example

1. Kids can learn to _____ between what they want and what they need.

2. Parents influence their children's attitudes toward money by

   _____ of responsible money management.

3. Kids can learn how to _____ and save even at a young age.

4. Parents can help kids _____ how long it will take to save the money to buy what they want.

5. Kids can learn how to _____ within their budget.

▶ Check your answers. Work with a partner and take turns reading your sentences.

▶ **B Sentence Form** Find five sentences in the reading that start with a verb and give advice. For example,

<u>Save</u> money for future schooling costs such as college tuition.
verb

▶ Write the sentence. Underline the verb.

1. _____

2. _____

3. _____

4. _____

5. _____

▶ Work with a partner and take turns reading your sentences. Give the meaning of the words you underlined.

Expanding Your Language

Reading

This reading expands on the idea of money and young people. Notice how much easier it is to understand this now that you have done some reading beforehand.

▶ First, read the following questions. After reading, answer them based on the information in the text.

1. What effect do young people have on today's economy?
2. Why are young people getting larger allowances?
3. How much do children affect their parent's purchasing decisions?
4. What types of direct marketing are aimed at young people?
5. How does the Internet play an important role in the youth market?
6. How can a young person make a purchase online?
7. What are the advantages and disadvantages of young people making purchases online?

The Youth Market Just Keeps on Growing

In North America, young people have gigantic buying power in today's economy. This has an effect on the media and on many companies that expect this market to increase their profits. First, the amount of money that teens have to spend is large and growing. The money they have comes from their allowances. The amount of money children receive for their allowance has increased by fifteen percent in the past ten years. Parents give their children large allowances when the economy is strong. Today, more parents are working. Their work keeps them so busy that they don't have enough time to shop with their children. Many parents are just too tired when they come home at the end of the day to discuss spending with their children. In fact, today many children influence their parents' decisions about what to buy for their family. Nine out of ten kids have some power over family spending decisions. Some researchers estimate that up to $565 billion of family purchases on such items as cars, furniture, vacations, and home entertainment items such as computers, telephones, televisions, and other technology are influenced by children.

Many companies are now marketing directly to young teens and pre-teens—especially girls. Major cosmetic and clothing manufacturers are producing brands that are attractive to a youth market. The clothes that young people want to buy are expensive—$150–250 for the latest-style blue jeans, $200 for a pair of shoes. The music and entertainment industries have traditionally marketed their products to the young, but now even the oldest of institutions—banks—are looking to this new market. They are promoting themselves to children as young as seven years old with special accounts and programs designed to teach them about savings and checking. Clearly, the youth market is important.

The Internet is another important part of the youth market. The percentage of kids under eighteen who are online is large and growing. It is estimated that kids ages five to eighteen will spend over $3 billion over the Internet. The amount of time that teens spend online is, on average, over seven hours a week. There are websites where teens can find out about anything they would like to buy. On some sites, kids can look at the latest fashions and personalize them by changing the size, color, or style to suit their taste. Internet purchases are easy because many young people have their own credit cards. Some companies have Internet-only debit accounts for their young customers to use. Kids deposit money into an account and then use the account number to make purchases on a website.

Of course, all of this offers parents and others a great opportunity to teach children about responsible attitudes toward money and consumption. Some studies show that the sooner kids learn how to budget, invest, and save money, the more successful they will be at avoiding debt later in life. But there are, of course, the dangers. Other studies suggest that kids typically spend ninety percent of the money they have, and their credit card debt is a problem that many parents have.

Learning how to budget and save money should start early. Living within our means is a lesson that should be learned at a young age and reinforced throughout our lives. Staying away from debt is better than getting out of debt. But in our consumer society, it isn't easy.

Speaking

▶ **Oral Presentations** Bring money from your country or another country of your choice. Prepare to talk about this currency to others in a small group. Present some interesting facts. For example, discuss different types of currency and their value, or describe any pictures or writing shown on the bills. Compare information with those who brought money from other countries.

▶ **Questionnaire** Answer these questions. Think about the reasons for your answers. Then interview two people and write their answers.

Your Answers	Person A	Person B
1. _____	_____	_____
2. _____	_____	_____
3. _____	_____	_____
4. _____	_____	_____

1. How would you describe your attitude toward money?
   a. I'm a spender.   c. I don't like to think about money.
   b. I'm a saver.   d. I'm worried I won't have enough.
2. How much do you think our personalities influence our attitudes toward money?
   a. Personality has a strong influence.
   b. Personality has some influence.
   c. Personality has little influence.
   d. Personality has no influence.

3. When did your current attitude toward money develop the most?

   a. Childhood   c. Adulthood

   b. Adolescence

4. How do people's needs for money change in the different periods of their life?

   a. Adolescence   c. Middle age

   b. Adulthood   d. Old age

Writing

▶ **Topic Writing** Choose one of the topics below or a topic of your own. Write as much as you can about your topic.

1. What are your ideas about the importance of money in society? How does your attitude compare with that of others you know?

2. At what age do you think young people should be allowed to work?

▶ Follow the writing instructions in Chapter 1 on pages 12 and 13.

 **Online Study Center**   For additional activities, go to the *Reading Matters* Online Study Center at *college.hmco.com/pic/wholeytwo2e*.

8 Lotteries: Good for Society?

▶ Chapter Openers

In-Class Survey

▷ Answer the following questions. Interview two other students in your class. Find out their opinion.

1. Why do people decide to buy lottery tickets?
2. What do you think the chances are of winning a lottery?
   a. Small
   b. Very small
3. Do the lives of lottery winners change?
   a. Yes, in a positive way.
   b. Yes, in a negative way.
   c. No, they do not change at all.
4. Should lotteries be advertised on television? Why or why not?
5. Have you ever bought a lottery ticket?
   a. Yes
   b. No

▷ Discuss your answers with a partner or in a small group. Share the information with the class.

Getting Information from a Graph

▷ Use the information in the graph on the next page to answer these questions.

1. Why do most people decide to buy a lottery ticket?
2. How do the results of this graph compare with what you found out in the survey?

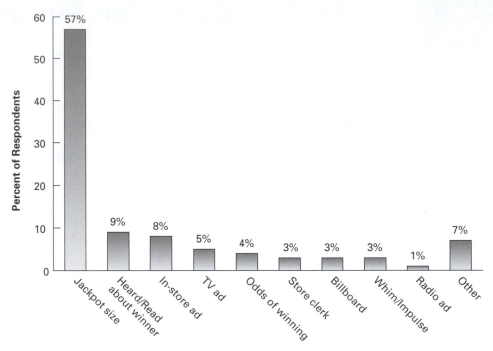

Reasons People Give for Buying Lottery Tickets

❯Paired Readings

▶ In this section, you will find two different stories on the same theme. Choose one of the two to work with. Prepare to explain the story to someone who read the same story and then to a person who read the other story.

Personalizing

▶ These are two very different stories about the experiences of people who have bought lottery tickets. Before reading your story, think about the positive and negative ways playing the lottery might affect you.

▶ List three positive or negative points of playing the lottery.

Positive	Negative
1. _____	_____
2. _____	_____
3. _____	_____

▶ Discuss your ideas with a partner.

Skimming

> Read your story and answer this question: Did the lottery players(s) in this story have a positive or a negative experience? Explain.

Positive: _____

Negative: _____

> Compare answers with a partner. Explain the reasons for your answer.

①Lottery Luck

Scanning

> Look for the answers to the questions after each paragraph. Underline the words in the paragraph that support the answer.

Against All Odds

❶   The town of Roby, Texas, is not a rich one. On average, individuals earn a little under $20,000 a year, and the population is only about 600. Most of the people are farmers. There aren't many well-paying jobs. In fact, most jobs pay only about minimum wage. The people in the town have had a lot of bad luck. They have experienced drought and falling prices for cattle. Many of the farmers have had serious financial trouble. Some families were worried that the banks were going to take away their farms. On Thanksgiving weekend in November 1997, many families felt unhappy as they sat down to their turkey dinner. Some thought that it would be the last Thanksgiving in their homes.

1. What two facts show that Roby, Texas, is not a rich town?

   a. _____

   b. _____

2. What kind of wage do most jobs pay?

   _____

3. What two problems have the farmers had?

   a. _____

   b. _____

4. Why were people unhappy at Thanksgiving?

   _____

---

❷   But over the Thanksgiving weekend, a miracle occurred. A group of forty-three townspeople each won part of a $46.7 million prize in the Texas state lottery. They won because they had all joined a lottery pool by putting in $10 each. They bought 430 tickets. Each person will take home about $40,000 a year, after taxes, for the next twenty years. The winners were very happy and grateful. Twenty-eight of the winners were farmers. They're not planning on taking any expensive vacations or buying enormous luxury homes. They plan to pay off the debts on their farms. One man said that the money will allow him to keep on farming instead of looking for a second job. Another said that he had been days away from giving up and leaving the town forever. The winners say that no one is planning to quit a paying job no matter how little money it brings. "Just now," said one, "I might think about buying a new pickup truck for the farm." But another man said that he and his wife wouldn't buy anything new. They plan to start saving money for college educations for their three children.

---

1. What miracle happened over the Thanksgiving weekend?

   _____

2. How did people join the lottery pool?

   _____

3. What did people win?

_____

4. What are two ways that people will use their money?

   a. _____

   b. _____

5. What are two ways that people will *not* spend their money?

   a. _____

   b. _____

---

❸   In the United States, lotteries are big business. There are lotteries in at least thirty-eight states and the District of Columbia. Americans spend more than $88 million every day in lottery games. In 2000, U.S. lotteries made a profit of $22 billion on sales of $45 billion. That makes lotteries the twenty-fourth largest company in sales in the United States. The lottery winners in Roby, Texas, are happy that they got involved in the lottery. Life will go on as it has for years in Roby, thanks in part to a bit of good lottery luck.

---

1. Where are there lotteries in the United States?

_____

2. How much money do Americans spend on lotteries every day?

_____

3. How much money do lotteries make every year:

   a. in sales? _____

   b. in profit? _____

▶ Compare answers with a partner. Try to agree on the same answers. Refer to the reading in cases where you disagree.

Recapping the Story

▶ List the facts of the story in note form.

Against All Odds

- Life in Roby, Texas
    - People earn a little under $20,000/year
    - Only about 600 people left in town
    -
    -
    -
    -
    -

▶ Work with a partner who took notes about the same story. Take turns explaining several of the facts to each other. Check to make sure that you both have the same information. Add any facts you didn't note. Correct any facts you need to.

Reacting to the Story

▶ Share your ideas about these questions with a partner.

1. Did the lottery winners in Roby use their winnings in a positive way?
2. Is the lottery an answer to people's financial problems?
3. Does this story show the positive or negative side of lotteries?

❷ Lottery Loss

Scanning   ▷ Look for the answers to the questions after each paragraph. Underline the words in the paragraph that support the answer.

Beating the Odds

❶   Andy D. (not a real name) was a successful businessman who owned a small restaurant. He was married and had two children. But he had a problem. He loved to gamble. He would spend his vacations and weekends gambling at the casinos. Because he made over $100,000 a year, he felt he could afford his one bad habit. Then, in 1992, Andy bought his first lottery ticket. He liked the idea of winning $1 million for a $1 investment. But, soon, he was spending up to $250 a day on lottery tickets. Andy was out of control. Over an eight-year period he estimated that he lost over $100,000 on lottery tickets. As Andy spent more and more on lottery tickets, his business began to fail. Finally, he lost his restaurant and his job and found himself over $1 million in debt. When his wife divorced him, he had to move in with his mother. But, as things got worse, his desire to win the lottery increased. He promised his son that he would get a job and get help. He promised his daughter that he would pay for her college tuition. He made promises but he couldn't stop gambling. Finally, on the day his daughter's tuition bill had to be paid, he stole some money from his mother and spent it trying to win at three different lottery games. He lost all of them. In despair, he tried to commit suicide.

1. Who is Andy D.?

   _____

2. What problem did he have?

   _____

3. How much money did he spend on lottery tickets?

   _____

4. What three problems did Andy's habit cause?

   a. _____

   b. _____

   c. _____

5. What did Andy try to do when he lost three lottery games?

   _____

❷   Andy was in a hospital for three weeks. The doctors and nurses helped him to recover from the suicide attempt. They encouraged Andy to join a self-help group, Gamblers Anonymous. With the help of this group, Andy began to change. Through the group, he got the support of professionals who helped him to find a job. He also got financial help. He made a monthly budget so that he could repay his debts. After six years, Andy began to see that he would be able to pay off the money he owed. Most importantly, Andy stopped buying lottery tickets. Today, he is able to help pay for his children's college tuition bills. The real reward for Andy is that his children believe in him and respect him. Andy is happy to know that he has won back his children's trust. He is beginning to realize that he can get the peace and happiness he always wanted without having to win a lottery.

1. How long was Andy in the hospital?

   _____

2. What did the doctors and nurses encourage him to do?

   _____

3. What two things did the group help Andy to do?

   a. _____

   b. _____

4. What three positive things have happened to Andy?

   a. _____

   b. _____

   c. _____

5. How does Andy feel about himself?

   _____

---

❸   As the story of Andy D. shows, lotteries cost more than just the spare change in people's pockets. Compulsive lottery gamblers will spend money, even steal money, to buy lottery tickets. This kind of addiction can lead to financial problems such as bankruptcy and job loss, health problems such as depression and suicide, and social problems that can include divorce and jail time for people who end up in court. The social cost of compulsive lottery gamblers can only be estimated. Some think the total amount could reach into the billions of dollars in the United States. In North America, the number of lotteries is increasing. Governments use this money to pay for things like education. The question remains: Are lotteries a good way for governments to raise money?

---

1. What are two things that compulsive lottery gamblers will do to buy tickets?

   a. _____

   b. _____

2. What are three types of problems that compulsive lottery gamblers can have? Give one example of each.

Type	Example
a. _____	_____
b. _____	_____
c. _____	_____

3. What is the total cost to society of people addicted to gambling?

_____

4. What question are people asking about lotteries?

_____

▶ Compare answers with a partner. Try to agree on the same answers. Look back at the reading if you disagree.

Recapping the Story

▶ List the facts of the story in note form.

Beating the Odds

- Andy D's life as a lottery gambler
  - successful businessman and restaurant owner
  - married and had two children
  - problem: loved to gamble
  -
  -
  -
  -
  -

▶ Work with a partner who took notes about the same story. Take turns explaining several of the facts to each other. Check to make sure that you both have the same information. Add any facts you didn't note. Correct any facts you need to.

Reacting to the Story

▶ Share your ideas about these questions with a partner.

1. What caused Andy D's problems?
2. How did he solve his problems?
3. Does this story show the positive or negative side of lotteries?

Comparing the Readings

Discussing the Stories

▶ **A** Work with a partner who took notes about the other story. Use your notes to retell the information.

▶ **B** Discuss the questions in the "Reacting to the Story" section for both stories.

▶ **C** Answer these questions based on the information from both stories.

1. What are the similarities and differences in the problems of the people in these two stories?
2. Is winning the lottery a solution to people's financial problems?
3. Are lotteries good or bad for society?

Vocabulary Building

Word Form and Meaning

▶ **A** Match the words in Column A with their meanings in Column B.

Column A

_____ 1. finance

_____ 2. individualize

_____ 3. invest

_____ 4. involve

_____ 5. occur

Column B

a. to make or do something specially for one person

b. to happen or take place

c. to include someone in something

d. to put time or money into something

e. to give money for something

▶ **B** Study these five words and their forms: verb, noun, adjective, and adverb. Then choose the correct form for each part of speech in the chart below. These words are commonly found in general and academic texts.

finance (v.)   individualize (v.)   invest (v.)   involve (v.)   occur (v.)
finance (n.)   individual   investment   involvement   occurred
financier (n.)   individually   investing   involved   occurrent
financial (adj.)   individual   invested   involvedly   occurrence
financially (adv.)   individualist   investor   involving

Verb	Noun	Adjective	Adverb
individualize	1. 2.	1.	1.
invest	1. 2.	1. 2.	
involve	1. 2.	1. 2.	1.
occur	1.	1. 2.	

▶ Compare lists with a partner. Try to agree on the same answers.

▶ **C** Write three or more sentences using words from the list.

▶ **D** Many words have more than one meaning. Look at these definitions for the word *control*.

a. **control (noun):** power to direct, guide, or manage

b. **control (noun):** an organization that manages an activity

c. **control (noun):** an experiment in which the subjects are treated in a parallel experiment

d. **control (verb):** to direct, guide, or manage an activity or person

▶ Read the sentences below and write the letter of the correct meaning on the line provided.

1. _____ He tried hard to **control** his gambling.

2. _____ She was a part of the **control** for an experiment to test the effectiveness of a new drug.

3. _____ The **control** she was looking for was hard to find.

4. _____ They acted as the **control** for the organization's work.

5. _____ The bank wanted to put **controls** in place to help the family save money.

E Matching Match each phrase in Column A with the word or phrase that is closest in meaning in Column B. Remember that when certain verbs and prepositions are combined they sometimes have special meanings.

Column A

_____ 1. give up

_____ 2. win back

_____ 3. move in

_____ 4. pay for

_____ 5. give back

_____ 6. pay off

_____ 7. end up

_____ 8. go on

_____ 9. take away

_____ 10. believe in

Column B

a. continue

b. return

c. trust

d. finish paying

e. remove

f. stop trying

g. regain

h. conclude

i. buy

j. occupy a home

Work with a partner to check your answers.

F Synonyms Circle the word that has the closest meaning to the word in boldface.

1. **allow**   punish   put   prohibit   permit
2. **estimate**   judge   know   value   desire
3. **leave**   enter   exit   excite   exhibit
4. **promise**   come   command   commit   combine
5. **realize**   underestimate   undergo   understand   underdone
6. **spend**   use for   use up   use instead   use with
7. **enormous**   very large   very small   very old   very new

Work with a partner to check your answers.

Expanding Your Language

Reading   This reading expands on the idea of the dangers of gambling. Notice how much easier it is to understand this now that you have done some reading beforehand.

▶ First, read the following questions. After reading, answer them based on the information in the text.

1. How did Angela develop an attraction to gambling?
2. What facts show that gambling is a growing problem for teens?
3. What is being done in schools to combat gambling?
4. Why are people unaware of the dangers of becoming addicted to gambling?
5. How successful has Angela been in curbing her gambling?

Teen Gambling: The Hidden Addiction

Angela was a true gambling addict at the age of seventeen. She picked up her first set of dice at age fourteen in breaks between her high school classes. Soon all she could think about was the idea of winning. She became so obsessed, in fact, that she would bet $200 on three tosses of the dice. Like most gamblers, she is unwilling or unable to say how much she lost in three years.

Youth gambling is a growing problem in the United States. Over the last thirty years, the number of kids gambling has increased dramatically. In a recent study, the Christian Science Monitor found that almost ninety percent of all high school seniors have gambled at least once. According to one professor, it is estimated that there are nine million adults in the United States who are addicted to gambling, and as many as one million teenagers. But even with these high numbers, there are no in-school programs in the United States that warn students of the dangers of gambling. Perhaps that is because many adults don't recognize that gambling can become an addiction. The spread of lotteries in stores, on video, and on the Internet make it an easy and often easily hidden activity.

Angela wants to stop but she recently gambled and lost $120 of the $200 her mother gave her to buy clothes. She hid her loss by changing the price tags on the clothes she bought. "Gambling is a disease," Angela says, "and it's not there for you to win, it's there for you to lose."

Writing

▶ **Reaction Writing** Think about the topic of lotteries and their effect on people. Are lotteries good or bad for society? Write about your ideas and any examples that you know of. For example, you can write about the different places where there are lotteries. What success and failure stories do you know?

Speaking

▶ **A Talk It Out** Work with a partner and tell each other about the ideas you wrote about. Begin by asking, "How do lotteries affect people in positive and negative ways?" Ask questions to find out more about your partner's ideas.

▶ **B Survey** Write four or five questions to survey some of your classmates and find out what they think about the role of lotteries in society. To review how to write a survey, see the example on page 87.

 *Online Study Center*   For additional activities, go to the *Reading Matters* Online Study Center at *college.hmco.com/pic/wholeytwo2e*.

9 The Future of Money

Chapter Openers

Discussion Questions

▶ Think about these questions. Share your ideas with a partner or a small group.

1. How do you like to purchase things: with cash, with a credit card, with a debit card, or by check?

2. a. What are some purchases you can't use a credit card or a debit card to make?

   b. What are some purchases you need a credit card or a debit card to make?

3. What are the benefits and dangers of using a debit card or a credit card to buy things?

4. Do you think that in the future you will use cash as much as or less than you do now?

Exploring and Understanding Reading

Predicting

▶ Circle *T* for true and *F* for false. Guess the answers to questions you are not sure of.

1. T   F   Debit cards can be used to buy items such as gas, movie tickets, and groceries.

2. T   F   Most workers receive their paychecks at work.

3. T   F   The government spends money every year to replace worn-out or damaged bills.

4. T   F   When people use debit cards to buy things, they sometimes spend more than if they paid in cash.

5. T   F   If your debit card is stolen, thieves can use it to take money from your bank account.

▶ Work with a partner. Compare your answers. You don't have to agree, but explain your reasons as completely as possible. After you finish reading, return to these questions and answer them based on the information you read.

Skimming

▶ Read the selection quickly and choose the statement that best expresses the general idea of the reading.

a. People use debit cards to purchase more of the things they need.
b. There are advantages and disadvantages to using debit cards instead of cash.
c. People who use debit cards instead of money get into debt more easily.

How Will You Be Paying?

❶   In the United States, it seems that we need money less and less these days. The amount of money, or currency as it is called, in circulation in the United States today is about $450 billion. But, because total yearly money exchanges amount to more than $4 trillion, we have to wonder why there is so little money circulating in the country. In fact, there is more U.S. currency circulating outside the country than inside. It turns out that one of the main reasons there is so little cash today is that Americans are making more and more business and banking transactions electronically. It is even possible to have two people exchange money, anywhere at any time, with a person-to-person electronic-payment system. Today, money is just information that is moved around by the computers that we depend on for so much in our society.

❷   We're paying for more and more things electronically. Debit cards can be used to pay for our gas, buy our movie tickets, and even purchase our groceries. In some places you can even use a card to pay for a taxi. You need a credit card to reserve a hotel room or rent a car. You can pay your bills from your home computer or at your banking machine (ATM) without ever using cash or writing a check. Since 2000, 100 million Americans have relied on direct deposit to receive payments or government benefits. The percentage of electronic transfers from bank accounts has risen every year since 2000, increasing 7.75 percent in one year to 3.3 billion transactions. During this time, the number of check and cash transactions rose only 1.9 percent. In the past, most workers received their paychecks at work. Now more than half of all U.S. workers have their paychecks deposited directly into their accounts. Ninety-seven percent of those workers say that they are very satisfied with the service.

❸   There are many advantages to using cards instead of money. You can buy things without having to bother to go to the bank first. But large institutions—banks, governments, and businesses—benefit the most from electronic banking. As of 2001, there were about 22 billion pieces of U.S. paper money in circulation. Paper money wears out or is damaged over time, so the U.S. government has to spend more than $250 million a year to replace it. Businesses have to spend time to count, store, and protect the money that is brought in. It costs a bank more money in time and administration to process checks than to carry out electronic transactions. Direct deposits do help individuals and organizations save on the costs of processing money. In 2000, more than $20.3 trillion in transactions were processed electronically. Direct deposit of checks prevents fraud, which can save business more than $10 billion each year. The U.S. government pays seventy-five percent of all Social Security recipients by direct deposit. It also pays the majority of its bills by computer. All of these savings in time and dollars add up.

❹   Of course, using cards instead of cash is not worry free. You sometimes have to pay a small service charge when you buy something with your card. And cards are easy to lose. There are a lot of cards left at the supermarket checkout counter. Some banks issue a card that doesn't need a PIN, or personal identification number, to make purchases. If such a card is stolen, thieves can quickly make charges on your account before you realize the card is gone. But, beyond security, money management experts are worried about the effect of cards on people's attitudes toward money. It is easier to give in to the impulse to buy when you can just pull out your card to make a purchase. It is easier to lose track of the amount of money you have in your budget or in your bank account and overspend when you use a debit card. If you're a spender by nature, you could get into debt more easily. Clearly, there is a lot to be careful about when it comes to using cards instead of money.

❺   Will we give up money for good and use "smart cards" in the future? The time when we won't need to carry money at all may be coming sooner than we think. But will this make our financial lives easier or not?

Recognizing Sub-points

> **Reading Tip**

Noticing that some information is more general (**sub-points** of the main idea) than other information (the **details**), is an important critical reading skill. ■

A sub-point is an idea that helps explain the writer's topic. This is an example:

People carry many different types of cards. One of these is credit cards.
         topic   sub-point

Credit cards can charge different interest rates.
        detail

▶ Circle *S* if the statement is a sub-point or *D* if the statement is a detail.

1. S D   The percentage of electronic transfers from bank accounts has risen every year since 2000, increasing 7.75 percent in one year to 3.3 billion transactions.

2. S D   We're paying for more and more things electronically.

3. S D   But large institutions—banks, governments, and businesses—benefit the most from electronic transfers.

4. S D   In 2000, more than $20.3 trillion in transactions were processed electronically.

5. S D   Another worry is losing your card.

6. S D   It is easier to lose track of the amount of money you have when you use a bank card.

Reacting to the Story

▶ Decide your opinion about the following questions.

1. Do electronic money transactions make us more or less independent:
   a. on a personal level?
   b. on a social level?
2. In this reading, do you think the author finds using cards rather than currency has more advantages than disadvantages?

▶ Give as many reasons and examples for your opinion as you can. Discuss your ideas with others in a small group. Share your ideas with your classmates.

Applying the Information

▶ **Developing Ideas** In Chapter 8, in the reading, "Beating the Odds," the writer uses the expression "spare change." Spare change is the money we carry in our wallet or leave on our desk. Find out how one person in the United States is making use of the money we sometimes overlook.

Pennies from Heaven

The U.S. Mint is working around the clock to resupply banks that have run out of pennies. It produces more than a billion pennies a month. Most of these pennies will go directly into people's penny jars, piggy banks, and under the sofa cushions in your living room. In fact, two-thirds of the pennies produced in the last thirty years have already dropped out of circulation. Banks and stores are busy thinking of ways to get people to bring in their pennies. Some suggestions include having stores "round off" their mechanized prices to make pennies unnecessary. But those pennies on top of your dresser may be worth more than you think. And now one person thinks she has found a cause that makes sending in all those pennies worthwhile.

A Chicago nun who asked folks to send in their pennies has gathered a total of $37,000—and the penny pot is still growing.

Sister Eileen says she began by asking friends, family, and former students for their unwanted pennies in order to reach her original goal of raising $20,000—or two million pennies.

But now Sister Eileen says she's shooting for enough pennies to pay for a new pickup truck, which the parish can use to retrieve bulkier donated items.

She says there are so many worthy causes out there that people have trouble deciding who to give their dollars to.

But when it comes to pennies, Sister Eileen says most folks consider them a nuisance and just want to get rid of them.

Discussion Questions

▶ Discuss the following questions with a partner or a small group.

1. Why does the U.S. Mint have to produce so many pennies?
2. Why do banks and stores need pennies?
3. Why is Sister Eileen asking people to send her their pennies?
4. Has her project been successful?
5. What does Sister Eileen say about people's attitude toward pennies?
6. What would happen to this kind of project in the age of electronic money?

Vocabulary Building

Word Form and Meaning

▶ **A** Match the words in Column A with their meanings in Column B.

Column A	Column B
_____ 1. credit	a. to change or bring about a change in something
_____ 2. process	b. to give ownership or recognition to someone or something
_____ 3. rely	c. to move someone or something to another place
_____ 4. secure	d. to depend on someone or something
_____ 5. transfer	e. to make someone or something safe

▶ **B** **Phrasal Verbs** Match each phrase in Column A with its meaning in Column B.

Column A	Column B
_____ 1. pay for	a. throw away
_____ 2. get rid of	b. overuse
_____ 3. shoot for	c. forget
_____ 4. wear out	d. buy
_____ 5. lose track of	e. happens as a result
_____ 6. turns out	f. try to get

▶ Use each phrase in a sentence of your own. Work with a partner and take turns reading your sentences.

▶ **C** Study these five words and their forms: verb, noun, adjective, and adverb. Then choose the correct form for each part of speech in the chart below. These words are commonly found in general and academic texts.

credit (v.)	process (v.)	rely (v.)	secure (v.)	transfer (v.)
credit (n.)	process	reliance	security	transfer
creditor (n.)	processed	reliant	secured	transferred
credit (adj.)	processing	reliably	securely	transference
credited (adj.)	processor	reliable	securer	transferable
	processing		secure	transferability

Verb	Noun	Adjective	Adverb
process	1. 2. 3.	1. 2.	
rely	1.	1. 2.	1.
secure	1. 2.	1. 2.	1.
transfer	1. 2. 3.	1. 2.	

▶ Compare lists with a partner. Try to agree on the same answers.

▶ **D** Write three or more sentences using words from the list.

Vocabulary in Context

▶ Complete each sentence with one of the words in the list. Use your understanding of one part of the sentence to help you guess the word that is missing. Circle the words that helped you decide your answer.

a. cost	b. count	c. deposit	d. give	e. process
f. received	g. reduce	h. rent	i. risen	j. stolen

1. You should call the bank if your card is lost or _____ and cancel the card immediately.

2. The employees had the company _____ their paychecks directly into their accounts.

3. After three weeks she finally _____ the money that they owed her.

4. The bank told her that it would take several days to _____ the checks and put the money into her account.

5. The auto rental company said she needed a credit card to _____ a car for the weekend.

6. It is a good idea to _____ the amount of money you owe on your credit card.

7. If you _____ all the money on my dresser, I have about fifteen dollars to spend.

8. Is it too late to _____ you the money to buy a ticket for tonight's concert?

9. The restaurant looked expensive, but she told me the meal wouldn't

   _____ a lot of money.

10. She said the price had _____ from $50 to $100 in just three years.

▶ Work with a partner and take turns reading your completed sentences.

Expanding Your Language

Reading

This reading expands on the idea of the dangers of credit. Notice how much easier it is to understand this now that you have done some reading beforehand.

▶ First, read the following questions. After reading, answer them based on the information in the text.

1. Why was Judy and Yves Donalds's wedding so expensive?
2. What facts show that weddings are becoming a financial problem for newly married couples?
3. Why are people influenced to have big weddings?
4. Why is it difficult for young couples to afford paying for their weddings?
5. What conflicts do young couples face starting out in their married life?
6. What benefit could come from managing debt for a newly married couple?
7. What happened to Judy and Yves?

In Debt at the Altar: A Wedding on Credit

There were a lot of expenses when the bills for Judy and Yves Donalds's wedding arrived. By the time the cost of the bride's wedding dress, the groom's tuxedo, the wedding cake and flowers, and a big wedding dinner for friends and family were added up, the Donalds were in over $15,000 worth of credit card debt. They had never been in such serious debt before.

Wedding debt is becoming an increasing problem for newlyweds in the United States. One credit management company says that, in 2002, close to 240 of its clients listed wedding spending as the main reason for their debt problems. Part of the reason for this increase may be the emotional factors involved. People tend to lose sight of finances when they are getting married. A recent survey of 1,400 bridal magazine readers found that forty-three percent spent more on their wedding than they had budgeted. Another factor is the cost of the wedding itself. An average wedding in the United States costs about $22,000. People feel that others expect them to have a fancy ceremony. Having a big wedding becomes a point of pride. Says one couple, "There is this idea that the big wedding is a good thing for everybody." An additional reason that weddings are creating debt is that more couples are paying for the weddings themselves. It's difficult to pay for a wedding at a point in people's lives when they are just starting out in their professions. It took one couple more than ten years to pay off the almost $6,000 in credit card debt they racked up because of their wedding.

Of course, starting out married life in debt adds to the potential for conflict between the new husband and wife. One couple said it added to the difficulties they had adjusting to living together. Another couple, however, said that dealing with their debt taught them patience. Paying off their wedding debt meant learning to wait on making other big purchases such as a second car, going out to restaurants, or taking out-of-town vacations. After five years, they finished making their final payment on their wedding debt. They've been married for eleven years and are only now planning for their first vacation. For Judy and Yves, the experience has not been as positive. After struggling with their debt for three years, they decided to separate.

Speaking

▷ **A Talk It Out** Work with a partner or with a small group of people from different countries. Find out how people do banking, make purchases, and pay bills in other places. Find out about people's attitudes toward money. Is it common for people to carry cash with them or to use credit cards? Do people think it's important to keep money in the bank? Ask questions to find out more about your partner's ideas.

▶ **B Debate** A debate is an exchange of ideas in which two people argue different and opposing views on a topic. "In the future we won't need to use cash; money will be a thing of the past." Do you agree or disagree with this statement? Work with a partner to think of and present reasons in favor of or against this statement. Prepare to talk for one to two minutes about your ideas. Practice explaining your point of view with your partner. When you are ready, present your point of view to someone who has a different view. Listen carefully and ask your partner who has an opposing view questions about the information. Share your ideas with your classmates.

Writing

▶ **A Topic Writing** Using the information in this chapter, write about the advantages and disadvantages of using cards instead of cash. Use examples of your own to help you explain your ideas.

▶ **B Reaction Writing** What does the story about Sister Eileen or Judy and Yves Donalds show you about attitudes toward money? Write about the different attitudes toward money that people have. Give as many details as possible.

Read On: Taking It Further

Newspaper Articles

▶ Check the newspaper over a few days and find an interesting article about lotteries or another money-related topic. Take notes as you did for the reading in Chapter 8, pages 94 or 98. Prepare to present the information to a partner or a small group.

Word Play

Reading Tip

Don't forget to write in your **reading journal** and add **vocabulary log** entries to your notebook. ▪

▶ **A Spelling Game** You can use vocabulary from the chapter readings to play this game. Think of a pair of words, like *loan* and *number*. The last letter of *loan* is the first letter of *number*. Select a partner and follow these rules to play the game.

▶ **1.** Make a list of seven to ten words from the readings that can be paired with another word.

2. Give your partner the first word to spell.

3. Your partner spells the word and must select a new word that begins with the last letter of the word spelled (one-minute time limit). If your partner can't find a word, you supply the answer.

4. Continue to take turns until time is called by the teacher (after approximately 10–15 minutes).

5. The person who correctly chooses and spells the most words wins.

Online Study Center   For additional activities, go to the ***Reading Matters*** Online Study Center at *college.hmco.com/pic/wholeytwo2e.*

UNIT 4

Protecting Nature

One generation goes, another generation comes, but the Earth remains forever.

—*Ecclesiastes 1:4*

Introducing the Topic

People have had an enormous effect on the natural world. Today, we know that we have to protect the natural world. This unit is about how we are struggling to protect our natural world for the future. Chapter 10 introduces you to new concerns about our night sky. You will learn about efforts being made to protect us from light pollution. In Chapter 11, you will find out what people are doing to protect wildlife. Should we bring wolves back to areas in the United States where they have been wiped out or are endangered? What should we do about wild animals that come too close to human habitation? Chapter 12 examines ways to protect our future supplies of fresh water.

Points of Interest

Descriptions

► Think about these statements. Free write your ideas. Share your ideas with a partner or in a small group.

1. What are some natural outdoor areas that you like, for example, beaches, forests, lakes, mountains, deserts, or rivers? Describe what is special about these wilderness areas. What do you like to do in these places?
2. Describe wild animals that you find interesting. Describe the places you would see these animals.

Questionnaire

► Read the following list of important reasons to protect nature. Check (✔) those that are important to you. Mark their order of importance from *1* (very important) to *5* (least important). Add any ideas of your own.

Reasons to Protect Nature	Importance
_____ Because we can relax when we're outdoors	_____
_____ Because it's important to future generations	_____
_____ Because we want to preserve the beauty of nature	_____
_____ Because it's good for the economy	_____
_____ Because it's important for science	_____
_____ Because it could be dangerous if we don't protect it	_____
Other: _____	_____

► Share your ideas with a partner or in a small group.

10 Night Light Pollution

▶Chapter Openers

Studying the Visuals

▷ Look at the following pictures of Los Angeles on the West Coast of the United States and answer the following questions.

Los Angeles basin from Mt. Wilson Observatory, 1908.

Los Angeles basin, 1988.

1. What do these pictures show?
2. When were these pictures taken?
3. What is the difference between the pictures from one time period to another?
4. What do you think could be the effect of this change on human beings? On animals?

Discussion Questions

▶ Think about these questions. Share your ideas with a partner or a small group.

1. a. What can you see in the night sky in the city?
   b. What can you see in the night sky outside the city?
2. What kind of outside lighting do you like to have at night in the city?
3. Do you think cities need more or less night lighting?
4. Do you like sleeping with a light on in your bedroom at night? Why or why not?
5. Is it important to our health to have daily periods of darkness and light? Why or why not?
6. Is it important for animals to have daily periods of darkness and light? Why or why not?

Exploring and Understanding Reading

Personalizing

▶ Imagine that you are going to interview an astronomer who is having trouble seeing the stars in the night sky because of artificial light coming from our cities. Write four questions that you might ask.

1. _____
2. _____
3. _____
4. _____

Skimming

▶ Quickly read the interview and circle the correct answer.

The astronomer
a. thinks light pollution is dangerous for humans.
b. thinks light pollution is dangerous for animals.
c. thinks light pollution is dangerous for both.

The Disappearing Darkness

In parts of the United States and Canada, night fall comes early in the spring, fall, and winter. At these times, homes and cities are ablaze with lights. Astronomers now report that ninety-seven percent of North Americans live under skies polluted by artificial light. Read an interview with one astronomer about the problem of light pollution.

Q: How do you know how bright the lights at night are?

A: We can see them from our observatories. There are billions of lights on Earth. Even at night, North America shines from space. And cities like New York, Washington, Toronto, and Montreal are among the brightest.

Q: Where does this light come from?

A: This light comes from a number of sources—highways, parking lots, sidewalks, and even our front doors. Most of us don't think about the effect that this outdoor light has. But that's because we only see what is right around us. The fact is, this light shines not only on the nearby ground where it is needed, but also miles away in the sky.

Q: What is the result of all this?

A: Well, for one thing, people today see only a small number of the stars in the sky. Let me give you an example of my own. I remember standing on my front steps at night as a child and being able to see far up into a sky filled with stars. That's an experience my children will never have. Some of the brightest comets of the century have come by in the last few years but people living in the cities haven't seen them.

Q: How much are people missing?

A: Well, in a natural night sky someone looking up should be able to see nearly 3,500 stars and planets and the glow from the Milky Way—our home galaxy. But in cities like New York or Montreal the number of visible stars has dropped to about 50. Ninety-seven percent of North Americans no longer see the Milky Way.

Q: Is it only affecting North America?

A: No, it's becoming a global problem. In fact, in the areas of the world where there are big cities, it no longer ever really gets dark at all. For instance, Italian and U.S. scientists who have published the first atlas of the world's artificial night-sky brightness found that night in eastern North America, Western Europe, Japan, and South Korea has become a constant artificial twilight that lasts until sunrise. Two-thirds of the world's population never see a truly dark sky. And in about ten percent of the world, it is never dark enough for people's eyes to become fully used to night vision.

Q: Why is there more light in the night sky than before? Is it the increase in population?

A: Well, partly that—more and more of the world's population is coming to the cities—but that's not the whole story. The other part is technology. For example, manufacturers are creating smaller and better lights that are many times brighter than we have ever had. And people and city governments are using these lights for streets, office buildings, malls, and homes. In most cases they are using more light than they need. Some experts estimate that about US $1 billion in lost and wasted light escapes into the atmosphere.

Q: Is there any other danger that we should know about?

A: Yes, light pollution could be harmful to our health.

Q: How?

A: Scientists in the United States are studying the possible links between night light and illnesses like depression, even cancer. Other doctors say it weakens our body's natural defenses. Our body needs a period of darkness at night. Without it, our immune system could be weakened.

Q: And I understand that light pollution is dangerous for animals.

A: For some animals, light pollution could be as dangerous as toxic chemicals or the destruction of their natural habitat.

Q: Why is this the case?

A: Darkness is important to animals, too. Artificial light can disturb reproduction. Other animals get confused by night light and end up getting hurt or even killed. Take the case of birds. Every year in Toronto, volunteers try to rescue thousands of birds that crash into lit-up offices at night. Still, millions aren't rescued. In Florida, sea turtles make their nests near the beach. Normally, newborn turtles walk from the nests into the sea. They need a dark night sky to find their way. But now the beach areas are lit up from the houses nearby. There is so much light that the turtles lose their way. They end up on the highway and die or are eaten by birds when the daylight comes.

Q: What can people do about this?

A: Individuals can replace their outside lights with lights that are directed down toward the ground and not up and out. They can put up a motion detector so that the light goes on only when someone is moving around outside. But city and state government can take action too. Some government officials are suggesting and passing laws to reduce the amount of light at night. In Alberta, for example, the city of Calgary is installing new street lamps to reduce light pollution. The province of Ontario recently declared a conservation area near Toronto a dark sky reserve—no night lights are allowed. It's the first in North America.

Q: Will this be enough?

A: No, light pollution is growing by ten percent every year. If we don't take this problem more seriously, soon we won't be able to tell the difference between night and day.

Understanding Explanations

In English, a common way to explain what you mean is to give an example. Special words, including **for example**, **for instance**, **like**, or **such as**, are used to introduce examples. The information in examples can help you to understand the general idea and elaborate on factual information. ▪

Look for the facts and examples to answer these questions.

1. What are the sources of the light we can see at night over populated areas of North America?

    _____

2. a. What effect does light pollution have on people today?

        _____

    b. What example does the astronomer give to explain this effect?

        _____

3. What facts show how little of the night sky is visible in

    a. North America?

        _____

    b. Europe, Japan, and South Korea?

        _____

4. a. How is technology putting more light into the night sky?

        _____

    b. How costly is this development?

        _____

5. What examples are given to show the effect of light pollution on human health?

    _____

6. What examples are given to show the effect of light pollution on animals?

    _____

7. What examples are given to show what individuals and governments can do to reduce the problem?

_____

_____

8. What fact shows how serious this astronomer think this problem is?

_____

▶ Compare answers with your partner. Try to agree on the same answers. Check the reading to confirm your answers.

Applying the Information

▶ **Skimming** This reading gives you some more information about one idea that the astronomer mentions in his interview. Read the article quickly and decide what this idea is.

Write what this reading is about in your own words.

_____

Saving the Sky

You Can Make a Difference

David Crawford thinks you can do a lot to save your sky and your electricity bill at the same time. Crawford is a professional astronomer, now retired, and in 1988 he helped begin the International Dark-Sky Association to reduce the amount of poor-quality lighting. First, he suggests that you make sure your outdoor lamps direct their light onto the ground, rather than spraying it upward or onto your neighbors' property. Point these lamps downward, use lower-wattage bulbs, and save a little on your electric bill! If 70 watts will do, why use 400?

Lights Around Your House

Reduce the strength of the lights you use outside. Some homeowners put bright bulbs in the fixtures near the entrances to their homes. They think that doing so improves visibility and safety. But the glare from a bright light actually lowers the ability to see well at night. This is because the pupils of your eyes get smaller in bright light even when everything else around you is dark. Also, very bright light will cast very dark shadows that could make it hard to see dangerous obstacles or people who are hiding there.

Stay Safe and Save Money: Use Motion Sensors

If you have a backyard security light that's constantly on, you may be causing a problem for yourself. This constant light only shows off your yard for passers-by or even would-be thieves to see. And these lights can be expensive to operate: As a rule of thumb, a security light that's on all night, every night, will cost you about $1 annually for every 2 watts of power used. For example, a 200-watt fixture will run up your electric bill by about $100 per year. One easy way to improve home security, cut your electric bill significantly, and reduce light pollution is to put motion sensors on your outdoor lamps. When the sensor triggers its light on, you'll know that something or someone is moving around outside. A security light activated by a motion sensor will be on at most a few times per night and cost you only a few dollars per year to operate. Most models have override switches to keep them turned on (or off) continuously if you wish.

Sweet-Talk the Neighbors

Perhaps the problem isn't in your yard but next door. You want to stop this wasteful, annoying light that's shining into your yard, but you also want to stay on good terms with your neighbors—so what can you do? The first and most important rule is to be polite. They obviously had reasons for putting that light up, so approach them in a friendly, understanding way. Crawford offers two approaches you can take to win them over. First, tell them about how much energy they are paying for without needing to. Maybe they got a good deal down at the store but don't realize that they'll spend far more on electricity than on the initial purchase. Second, explain that such a bright, glaring light is actually counter-productive to good nighttime vision—theirs and yours.

Seeing is Believing

One of the best ways Crawford raises local awareness about lighting is by inviting the neighbors over for a look through one of his telescopes. Every Halloween, the neighborhood kids (and their parents!) stop by for two treats: something sweet for the tongue and something amazing for the eye. This gets everyone thinking about the night sky and how light pollution threatens it. Light pollution can be minimized, but getting there will take a real effort by everyone who loves the night sky. As Crawford asks, "If not you, then who? If not now, when?"

Note Taking   ▶ **Listing Solutions** List four ways to reduce light pollution. Note the facts such as reasons or explanations for each one.

Ways	Reasons/Explanations
1.	
2.	
3.	
4.	

▶ Work with a partner and take turns comparing the facts you chose. Work with your partner to add as many facts as possible to your list. Check your facts with your classmates.

◗ Vocabulary Building

Word Form and Meaning   ▶ **A** Match the words in Column A with their meanings in Column B.

Column A

_____ 1. manufacture

_____ 2. minimize

_____ 3. publish

_____ 4. threaten

_____ 5. trigger

Column B

a. to put someone or something in danger

b. to print or issue something

c. to begin or start something

d. to produce or make something

e. to decrease something or make it smaller or less important

▶ **B** Study these five words and their forms: verb, noun, adjective, and adverb. Then choose the correct form for each part of speech in the chart below. These words are commonly found in general and academic texts.

manufacture (v.)	minimize (v.)	publish (v.)	threaten (v.)	trigger (v.)
manufacturer (n.)	minimization	publication	threatened	triggered
manufactured (adj.)	minimal	published	threatening	trigger
manufacturing (adj.)	minimally	publisher	threateningly	triggering
	minimum	publishable	threat	
	minimum			

Verb	Noun	Adjective	Adverb
minimize	1. 2.	1. 2.	1.
publish	1. 2.	1. 2.	
threaten	1.	1. 2.	1.
trigger	1.	1. 2.	

▶ Compare lists with a partner. Try to agree on the same answers.

▶ **C** Write three or more sentences using words from the list.

▶ **D** Choose the correct word to complete the sentences. Use your knowledge of grammar rules (i.e., if the word is a noun, adjective, verb, or adverb) to help you choose.

1. pollute / pollution

   a. I understand that there has been a big increase in light _____.

   b. I know that the high wattage bulbs sold in all the stores _____.

2. population / populated

   a. This area is one of the most _____ in North America.

   b. There are many reasons the _____ of cities in North America has grown.

3. experience / experienced

   a. I know that you don't have to be an _____ astronomer to know something about the stars in the night sky.

   b. I want to have my children _____ the wonder of seeing the stars in the night sky.

4. reproduce / reproduction

   a. Artificial light can disturb _____.

   b. Turtles _____ on the beaches where they build their nests.

5. estimate / estimated

   a. Scientists now _____ that about $1 billion a year is lost on wasted light.

   b. Scientists think that the number of stars it's _____ people can see is far less now than a decade ago.

▶ Check your answers. Work with a partner and take turns reading your sentences.

▶ **E Antonyms** Match each word in Column A with its antonym (a word that has an opposite meaning) in Column B.

Column A

_____ 1. bright

_____ 2. install

_____ 3. weaken

_____ 4. outdoor

_____ 5. rescue

_____ 6. toxic

_____ 7. sweet

_____ 8. productive

_____ 9. minimize

_____ 10. significant

_____ 11. reduce

_____ 12. natural

Column B

a. increase

b. unimportant

c. dark

d. counter-productive

e. artificial

f. sour

g. strengthen

h. harmless

i. maximize

j. indoor

k. endanger

l. remove

▶ Write three or more sentences using words from the list.

Vocabulary in Context

▶ **Jigsaw Sentences** The words *but* and *however* are used to express an idea that is different in some way from another idea in the same sentence. Match the beginning of the sentence in Column A with the best completion of the sentence in Column B.

Column A

_____ 1. This light shines not only on the nearby ground

_____ 2. Some of the brightest comets have come by

_____ 3. Perhaps the problem isn't in your yard

_____ 4. Maybe they got a good deal at the store

_____ 5. Light pollution can be minimized

Column B

a. but it will take real effort from everyone.

b. but it's coming from the house next door.

c. but also miles into the sky.

d. but city people haven't seen them.

e. but didn't realize how much they'd spend on electricity.

▶ Work with a partner. Look at the readings to check your answers. *But* and *however* can also begin sentences. Circle other sentences you find where *but* or *however* is used. What ideas are contrasted?

Expanding Your Language

Reading

This reading is about one man who watches the night sky and the work he does to bring the pleasure of that experience to others. Notice how much easier it is to understand this now that you have done some reading beforehand.

▶ **A** First, read the following questions. After reading, answer them based on the information in the text.

1. a. When did John Dobson first become interested in the stars?
    b. How long has he remained interested in the stars?
2. How did Dobson invent his first telescope?
3. What did he discover he could see with his invention?
4. What did he do in San Francisco?
5. a. What organization did he begin?
    b. What does this organization do?
6. What is the best part of his lectures?
7. What are the members of Dobson's class making?
8. How do people respond to seeing through Dobson's telescopes?
9. Why does Dobson believe that small telescopes are important?
10. How does Dobson feel about the relationship of the earth to the sky?

The Joys of Stargazing

Eugene, Ore.—When he was a child growing up in Beijing, John Dobson used to lie on his back, look upward, and imagine the sky was a vast ocean below him. If only he could leave the earth, he wondered, how far would he be able to dive into the sky's endless depths?

Mr. Dobson has never stopped wondering about what lies beyond our home planet. After his parents—both teachers—returned to San Francisco from China in 1927, Mr. Dobson studied chemistry at the University of California at Berkeley. Now, almost ninety years old, Mr. Dobson is one of history's greatest popularizers of science. He began the Sidewalk Astronomers of America, invented a simple, cheap, yet powerful telescope, has been on many programs (he's appeared on "The Tonight Show," PBS, and dozens of radio programs), and hosted "star parties." Mr. Dobson still travels all over the world, teaching all the time. He has brought the wonders of the universe to millions. In one summer alone, he taught weeks-long classes in telescope making and cosmology in Texas, Oregon, and New York. Then, after a trip to Italy and a brief stay in his San Francisco basement apartment—his "home" for only a few weeks each year—he's off to South America.

He first invented his telescope in the early 1950s. He noticed a twelve-inch piece of thick rounded glass on a friend's table and realized that it could be polished with sand into a reflecting telescope mirror. Then he mounted it with ordinary materials of wood and cardboard. When he pointed his homemade telescope at the moon, he was astonished by how much detail he could see. He could see the mountains and valleys on the surface as clearly as if he were about to land. Mr. Dobson started lending telescopes to kids who'd see him stargazing on the streets of San Francisco, and then began teaching them to make their own. Eventually, in 1968, he co-founded the Sidewalk Astronomers. He worked in an old school bus that made hundreds of trips around California for star parties. There are now two dozen chapters in places such as Sao Paulo, Liverpool, Moscow, and British Columbia. And Mr. Dobson lives a simple life, staying with members and friends on his travels around the world, teaching people to build telescopes and to understand what they see with them.

His lectures are filled with facts and theories, but the best part is what happens after his lecture. The audience moves outside to find a dozen or more telescopes set up and pointing at the evening sky. The members of the telescope class Mr. Dobson has been teaching for the past month are showing off their new scopes, assembled for a few hundred dollars from hardware-store components. (A "Dobsonian" can be made for as little as $20.) They've been setting up on busy street corners for the past week, drawing crowds of curious viewers young and old. Some of the cylinders stretch to eight feet long and more than a foot in diameter. "Awesome!" cries one teenager. "Wow!" marvels another. Despite the availability of recent TV and Internet images of Saturn's rings, passers-by and students alike are clearly amazed by what they can see through a telescope lens: Jupiter's bands, other galaxies, and a three-quarter moon whose surface is so distinct it seems you could almost spot the American flag at Tranquility Base.

Just as the young Mr. Dobson was able to see the sky as an ocean below him, what he really wants viewers to see through their telescopes is a new way of looking at the universe. And he has another reason. The fact is that small scopes can make big discoveries, like the planet discovered recently in a constellation 500 light years from Earth by astronomers using a four-inch telescope (a third the diameter of some of these), or the nebula spotted by a Kentucky amateur astronomer's three-incher in January, 2004.

Recently a puzzled park ranger, spotting Mr. Dobson leading one of his frequent star parties at Yellowstone National Park, asked the old stargazer if he considered the sky to be part of the park. "No," he replied, "the park is part of the sky."

Speaking

▶ **A** **Reacting to the Story** Discuss the following questions in a small group.

1. Why are the people in these stories so interested in the night sky?
2. What about the night sky attracts you? Where would you go to look at it?
3. What names or stories do people have for what they see in the sky?

▶ **B** This is a story about a man with a passion who dedicated his life to transmitting that passion to others and sharing it with as many people as he could. Think of a person whose passion inspired you. Write a few notes about that person. Share with others in a small group.

Writing

▶ **A** **Explaining Advantages** Make a list of facts you have gathered from the readings in this chapter to write about the advantages of preserving the night sky. Give examples to explain your ideas.

▶ **B** **Reaction Writing** Using your speaking notes, write about a person with a story that inspired you. Include details about the person's life, his/her passion, the ways he/she shares that passion, and the reasons for doing so.

 *Online Study Center*   For additional activities, go to the *Reading Matters* Online Study Center at *college.hmco.com/pic/wholeytwo2e*.

11 The Return of the Wolves

▷ Chapter Openers

Discussion Questions

▷ Think about the following questions. Share your ideas with a partner or a small group.

1. What do you know or think about wolves?
    a. What do wolves look and act like?
    b. Where do wolves live?
    c. What do wolves like to eat?
    d. What stories do people tell about wolves?
2. What positive or negative feelings do you have about wolves?
3. If wolves are endangered, should they be protected?

▷ Paired Readings

▷ In this section, you will find two different stories on the same theme. Choose one of the two to work with. Prepare to explain the story to someone who read the same story and then to a person who read the other story.

① Wolves in the Wild

Skimming

▷ Read the selection and circle the answer to the following question.

Has the reintroduction of wolves to Yellowstone
National Park been successful?   Yes   No

▷ Work with a partner. Explain the reasons for your answer.

Understanding Details

▷ Answer the questions after each paragraph. Underline the words in the reading that support the answer.

Wolves in Yellowstone National Park

❶   Yellowstone National Park is a wilderness area located in the western United States. The Rocky Mountains run through the park. The park has 2.3 million acres of mountains, river valleys, and forests. Every year visitors come here to see one of the last completely wild places in the United States. The park today is home to many wild animal populations, such as elk, buffalo, and bear. In the past another wild animal—the gray wolf—lived here in large numbers. In fact, there used to be many wolves in the United States. It is estimated that, in the 1600s, gray wolf populations could be found in areas from northern Mexico to Greenland. But wolves were killed when people moved in and settled the United States, so that by 1870, the gray wolf population was falling rapidly. In the 1920s, the last gray wolves were hunted down and completely eliminated from Yellowstone National Park. Since that time, environmentalists have wanted to see the return of wolves to Yellowstone. In 1973, the U.S. government passed a law that made it possible. In 1982, the U.S. Fish and Wildlife Service first suggested a plan to move ten breeding pairs of wolves to the park. Then, in 1995, fourteen Canadian gray wolves were brought to Yellowstone. More were introduced in the following year, bringing the number to thirty-one. Now there are almost 250 wolves that populate the park. The last of the original group of Canadian wolves died in February 2004, so all of the remaining wolves are native to the park.

1. Where is Yellowstone National Park located? How large is it?

   _____

2. What kinds of animals can you find in the park?

   _____

3. What area did gray wolves inhabit in the 1600s?

   _____

4. What happened to gray wolves in the United States and in Yellowstone National Park by 1920?

   _____

5. What has happened since the 1970s to return wolves to Yellowstone?

   a. 1970s _____

   b. 1980s _____

   c. 1990s _____

   d. 2000s _____

---

❷   When the wolves were first reintroduced in 1995, there were some doubts about whether this plan would work. First, some Canadians were unhappy about the removal of these animals from their natural habitat. They were worried that the animals might die as a result of the move. They were also worried that the wolves would be killed by hunters or ranchers in the United States. On the other hand, the hunters were concerned that wolves would prey on the elk and kill so many that there wouldn't be enough left for them to hunt. Ranchers and farmers who live in the area near Yellowstone argued against returning wolves to the area. From their point of view, these wolves were dangerous because they hunt their livestock, the cattle and sheep that feed in pastures next to the park. Some ranchers and farmers said that wolves could attack small children and domestic animals, such as dogs who live near the park. Many people simply felt that the federal government should not be spending the taxpayers' dollars to return the gray wolves to Yellowstone. However, the program has proven to be a success. The wolves have not preyed on livestock. In fact, coyotes killed twenty-eight times more sheep and lambs in 2002 than wolves did. Wolves do hunt elk but have not harmed the population; in fact, scientists see some beneficial changes to the ecosystem. Before the wolves, the elk would eat willow trees by the river banks. The willows were disappearing. Now with the danger of wolves preying on them, the elk are too nervous to spend a long time in open stream beds. They drink and move on quickly, no longer staying by the river bank to eat the young trees.

1. What happened in 1995?

_____

2. Why were some Canadians unhappy about the removal of the wolves?

    a. _____

    b. _____

3. What are three reasons that hunters, ranchers, and farmers didn't want wolves returned to Yellowstone National Park?

    a. _____

    b. _____

    c. _____

4. How has the return of the wolves to Yellowstone disproved people's fears?

_____

❸   Biologists are now able to observe the role that wolves play in the ecosystem of this wilderness area. In Yellowstone they can watch packs of wolves as they go about their daily lives. Through the aid of technology, they can observe the full range of their behavior, from hunting to raising their young. Many of the wolves have a collar that contains a global positioning receiver. Twice a day a satellite fixes the position of the animal and the data is stored on its collar. Later, researchers can find the wolf and come close enough to it to download the information to their laptop computer. Scientists have learned new facts about how wolves hunt. Not all wolves are good at hunting. There are only about two or three hunters in any pack of animals. It takes many attempts to kill an elk. Only one in four attempts is successful. And they've observed that wolves are patient hunters. Wolves will watch for hours until an animal makes a fatal mistake. Then they move. But even then, hunting is risky for wolves. Biologists have documented eight cases of wolves that have been killed by their prey. Biologists are learning that the lives of wolves are more complicated than they ever knew. They believe that Yellowstone is benefiting from the reintroduction of these animals. And biologists are not the only witnesses to the mysterious lives of wolves. The landscape of the park, with its open grassy meadows, makes it possible for visitors to observe these animals with ease. Visitors to the park can have the experience of hearing wolves howl at night—an experience many describe as the best the wilderness has to offer.

1. How are scientists able to follow the wolves?

   _____

2. What new information have they learned about the wolves as hunters?

   a. _____

   b. _____

3. What problems do wolves have hunting elk?

   a. _____

   b. _____

4. What experiences of the wolves can visitors have?

   a. _____

   b. _____

> **Reading Tip**

Highlighting is a useful strategy for finding and remembering facts and important ideas you read. To highlight, use a colored highlighting pen to mark information. Be careful to **mark only** the **words and phrases** that you want to stand out—not the whole sentence. Use the underlining you did to answer the scanning questions to help you locate the correct information to highlight. ■

▶ Compare answers with your partner. Try to agree on the same answers. Look back at the reading if you disagree.

Recapping the Information

▶ **A Highlighting** Highlight the facts you read about wolves relating to these ideas:

1. History of wolves in Yellowstone
2. Doubts about introducing wolves in Yellowstone
3. Experience of introducing wolves in Yellowstone

▶ **B Pair Work** Compare your highlighting with your partner's. Add any highlighting you need to. Using the highlighting, tell the important facts of the story.

Reacting to the Information

▶ Discuss this question with a partner.

What facts do you think countered the arguments of people who opposed the return of wolves to Yellowstone National Park?

❷ The Wolves Next Door

Skimming

▶ Read the selection and circle the answer to the following question.

Do wolves need to have wilderness areas to live?   Yes   No

▶ Work with a partner. Explain the reasons for your answer.

Understanding Details

▶ Answer the questions after each paragraph. Underline the words in the reading that support your answers.

The Unknown Lives of Wolves

❶   Wolves are among the most mysterious of wild animals in North America. They are strong animals with powerful jaws. They've been known to track, or follow, animals for many miles. But, despite the popular image, wolves do not needlessly attack and kill other animals. They look for the old, sick, and weak animals in a herd and target them in order to minimize the danger to themselves that could come from attacking a strong healthy animal. In one study of wolf behavior, scientists recorded wolves following moose 131 times. In these hunts, wolves attacked only seven times and killed only six times. Animals can and do defend themselves against wolves. In fact, wolves have been killed by the animals they hunt. Wolves travel in small groups called "packs." On average, a pack is made up of a dominant female and a dominant male, several males and females, and pups (wolf babies) that are raised by all the adults. Usually, only the dominant male and female mate. Again, contrary to popular belief, the pack is led not by the dominant male but by the dominant female. The females mark the pack's territory. Often the females break the snow and lead the pack on the hunt.

1. What is the difference between the popular image of wolves as hunters and the reality?

    _____

2. What important facts have scientists learned about how wolves hunt moose?

    _____

3. What is the makeup of a wolf pack?

    _____

4. What role do the females play in the life of the pack?

    _____

❷   When people think of wolves, they think of forests and areas far away from where there are large human populations. That's why it is so surprising that scientists in Wisconsin have discovered that wolves can cope with people. Unlike the wolf population in Yellowstone National Park, the wolves in Wisconsin live in areas that are close to human populations. One surprising discovery is that the wolves in Wisconsin have come back from being an endangered population of about 25 in the 1970s to numbering over 350 wolves today. These wolves are smaller than the ones in Yellowstone National Park. They weigh between 50 and 100 pounds. The top weight for wolves is 150 pounds. The wolves have come back on their own without any special programs to help them. They have increased their numbers in an environment that includes woods and some forests but has farms and pasture land as well. Their territory is close to human population centers. In fact, one pair of wolves was sighted only a two-hour drive away from the Mall of America in Bloomington, Minnesota. There are now more than 3,000 wolves in the areas of Minnesota, Michigan, and Wisconsin. These numbers grew after the Endangered Species Act was passed in 1973. It protected the wolves from being trapped or shot by hunters. The growth in the wolf population demonstrates that these animals can co-exist with others in an environment that is not purely wilderness.

1. What is the difference between the territories where wolf packs in Wisconsin live and those where the wolves live in Yellowstone?

_____

2. How does the size of wolves in Wisconsin compare with that of those in Yellowstone?

_____

3. How close do the wolves come to human populations? What is surprising about this?

_____

4. How did the wolves in Wisconsin grow to such numbers? What does this prove?

_____

❸   In Wisconsin, wolves prey on deer and other wild animals such as beaver and coyote. Of course, wolves often come across livestock such as cattle, sheep, turkeys, and chicken. The state government gives compensation to anyone who suffers property damage because of endangered species. In 2002, it paid $602 for each calf killed by a wolf. But wolves also kill dogs. A hunting dog is very expensive. There have been cases where the state has paid $2,500 to a dog owner whose animal was killed by a wolf. The highest amount of compensation so far has been $48,000. This payment was made to a game farm rancher to compensate for the loss of deer he raises for hunters who want to kill trophy deer. Scientists are studying the wolves to find out what risk factors lead to animals being killed. So far, they have found that when the wolf population grows, it is the younger wolves that start new packs. These young wolves are more likely to look for new areas to live in. This could bring them closer to pasture and farm land. Also, an increased number of deer will draw these animals to new territory. If a wolf returns to a farm or ranch, it is first relocated. If it returns again, it is removed and killed. Scientists are conducting research to uncover the conditions that bring wolves into dangerous contact with livestock. Their goal is to help the officials who protect the wolves know where to put their efforts for control and to develop new ideas for keeping the wolves away from prey that will cause them trouble.

1. What do wolves prey on?

   _____

2. What are some cases in which the government has paid compensation for animals that wolves killed?

   _____

3. How do wolves move into new territory? What problems can this cause?

   _____

4. What work are scientists doing? What is their goal?

   a. _____

   b. _____

▶ Compare answers with your partner. Try to agree on the same answers. Look back at the reading if you disagree.

Recapping the Information

▶ **A Highlighting** Highlight the facts of these ideas about wolves.

1. Characteristics of wolves
2. Wolves in Wisconsin
3. Wolves as predators in Wisconsin

> **Reading Tip**

See page 134 for tips on **highlighting**. ◼

▶ **B Pair Work** Compare your highlighting with your partner's. Highlight any important facts you didn't include. Using the highlighting, tell the important facts of the story.

Reacting to the Information

▶ Discuss these questions with a partner.

1. Can wolves be protected in areas near human populations?
2. Do the facts show that wolves are dangerous to other animals and humans?

Comparing the Readings

Discussing the Information

▶ Work with a partner who took notes about the other story. Use your notes to retell the information.

▶ Quickly tell your partner about the important facts you highlighted. Explain the ideas clearly in your own words. Encourage your partner to ask questions about the information or note some of the important facts you explain. Together discuss the questions in "Reacting to the Information."

Applying the Information

▶ **Using Facts to Make an Argument**   The wolves have come back after being reintroduced in Yellowstone and have also come back in Wisconsin. As you have learned, at one time wolves could be found throughout many parts of the United States. Now the situation is changing. Should wolves continue to be protected by the Endangered Species Act in areas such as Wisconsin where they have returned? What facts can you use to support your opinion?

To prepare and present your argument, complete the following steps:

▶ **1.** Choose an argument either for or against allowing wolves to continue to be protected by the Endangered Species Act.

2. Work together in a small group of people who share your opinion. Include people who prepared both readings in the group. Use the facts from both readings to find support for your argument. Add facts of your own to make your arguments stronger.

3. Make a final list of all the facts you can use. When you have completed your list, practice presenting your arguments with a partner.

4. Work with a partner who prepared the opposite argument. Take two minutes each to present your case. Listen to your partner's argument. Write the facts of your partner's argument in note form.

5. With your classmates, make a list of all the arguments for and against maintaining endangered species status. Ask and answer any questions about the facts of the case. As a class, try to agree on what you think the court decision should be.

◗Vocabulary Building

Word Form and Meaning

◗ **A** Match the words in Column A with their meanings in Column B.

Column A

_____ 1. compensate

_____ 2. conduct

_____ 3. document

_____ 4. dominate

_____ 5. eliminate

Column B

a. to carry out or lead something

b. to control or rule over someone or something

c. to remove or get rid of something

d. to pay someone or make up for something

e. to record or report something

◗ **B** Study these five words and their forms: verb, noun, adjective, and adverb. Then choose the correct form for each part of speech in the chart below. These words are commonly found in general and academic texts.

compensate (v.)	conduct (v.)	document (v.)	dominate (v.)	eliminate (v.)
compensation (n.)	conductor	documented	dominating	elimination
compensatory (adj.)	conductible	document	dominant	eliminator
compensative (adj.)	conductibility	documentary	domination	eliminated
compensatorily (adv.)	conduction	documentation	dominating	eliminating
	conductive	documentary	dominantly	

Verb	Noun	Adjective	Adverb
conduct	1. 2. 3.	1. 2.	
document	1. 2. 3.	1. 2.	
dominate	1. 2.	1. 2.	1.
eliminate	1. 2.	1. 2.	

◗ Compare lists with a partner. Try to agree on the same answers.

▶ **C** Write three or more sentences using words from the list.

▶ **D** Many words have more than one meaning. Look at these definitions of the word *conduct*.

a. **conduct (noun):** manner of carrying oneself
b. **conduct (verb):** to lead or direct an activity such as an orchestra
c. **conduct (verb):** to act or behave in a certain way
d. **conduct (verb):** to carry information in a channel

▶ Read the sentences below and write the letter of the correct meaning on the line provided.

1. _____ The president reminded them that the way they **conduct** themselves sends an important message about who they are.

2. _____ The connection allows them to **conduct** the electricity directly to the equipment.

3. _____ It would be hard to question her **conduct** because it was so honest.

4. _____ He showed by his **conduct** that this was important to him.

5. _____ The maestros lose themselves in their work when they **conduct** their orchestras.

▶ **E** In English, the form of a word can be changed. One of the ways is to add a special suffix, or word ending. The suffixes *-tion*, *-ion*, or *-sion* can be added to certain verbs to form nouns.

▶ Choose the correct word to complete the sentences. Use your knowledge of grammar rules to help you make the right choice.

1. consult / consultation

   a. The ranchers wanted to know if the government would _____ with them.

   b. They made a plan to meet ranchers and be available for _____ with them.

2. discuss / discussion

   a. They decided that a lot of _____ was needed to find out people's opinions.

   b. They decided that they would _____ their difference of opinion.

3. eliminate / elimination

 a. The original settlers wanted to see the total _____ of the wolf population.

 b. The original settlers wanted to _____ wolves because they thought they were dangerous.

4. oppose / opposition

 a. They told the government they would _____ this plan.

 b. They told the government there was a lot of _____ to this plan.

5. introduce / introduction

 a. They planned for the _____ of six pairs of animals into the park.

 b. They planned to _____ six pairs of animals into the park.

6. weigh / weight

 a. The wolves _____ between 50 and 100 pounds.

 b. The top _____ for wolves is 150 pounds.

▶ Work with a partner and take turns reading your sentences.

▶ **F Past Tense Verbs** Write the past tense of the following verbs. Circle these verbs in the readings.

1. attack   _____

2. document   _____

3. introduce   _____

4. move   _____

5. protect   _____

6. raise   _____

7. settle   _____

8. suggest   _____

▶ Check your answers. Write three sentences and three questions of your own, using past forms of any of these verbs.

❱Expanding Your Language

Reading

This reading is about Luna, a killer whale that has come very close to shore—too close, some say, for safety. Notice how much easier it is to understand this now that you have done some reading beforehand.

▶ **A** First, read the following questions. After reading, answer them based on the information in the text.

1. Where and when does this story take place?
2. What problems have occurred that worried people?
3. Why is Luna's behavior unusual for a killer whale?
4. What did scientists plan to do with Luna?
5. How would scientists carry out their plan?
6. Why did scientists want to do this?
7. What possible problems could arise?
8. a. What other case of killer whale/human contact has there been?
   b. What happened to the killer whale in this case?

▶ **B** Discuss your answers with a partner or with others in a small group.

Luna the Orca

In the summer of 2001, a young male orca, or killer whale, entered Nootka Sound in British Columbia, on the west coast of Canada, and went close to boats and planes in the harbor area. In the summer of 2003, news reports showed that the whale, named Luna, came so close to humans that they could touch and even feed the animal. Some reports even suggested that the animal was being hurt by people's careless behavior. One woman was fined $100 for petting the whale. The whale caused some problems when it damaged a boat's rudder, leaving it unable to steer home. People were afraid that it could flip a boat.

No one knows why Luna stayed in the sound. He appeared to have left his pod, which is unusual behavior for a killer whale. Killer whales are tightly-knit communities which are stable and stay together for their lives. In the two and a half years since arriving in the harbor, Luna never tried to swim back to the open ocean.

But in the coming spring, scientists planned to scoop Luna out of the water, put him in a special sleeve, and transport the animal back to its relatives by truck. At the southern tip of Vancouver Island, in a bay near the Juan de Fuca strait that separates Vancouver Island from Washington State, the scientists would keep Luna until his pod shows up as it does each summer. Then they would release the animal. It is an expensive trip back to the family, costing at least half a million dollars. Nearly half of that money would come from U.S. and Canadian taxpayers. The rest would, hopefully, come from donations.

The scientists thought that it was important to have Luna rejoin his pod. They put an electronic monitor on the animal in hopes that they would find out where the animals go in the winter. But, there was a chance that the reunification would not occur. Luna's mother had another calf and might not even recognize the prodigal son. The pod could turn on Luna and attack him. It would take at least a week before scientists know if they were successful.

This is not the first time that scientists have tried to return an orca whale to a wild population. In December 2003, the killer whale Keiko, the star of the movie "Free Willy," died of pneumonia in a Norwegian fjord, two years after he was returned to the wild. Although he was taught to catch his own fish and interact with other wild orcas, Keiko never lost his taste for human companionship. He swam toward a small coastal town in Norway and would approach small boats and invite people to enter the water with him.

Speaking

▶ **A Two-Minute Taped Talk** Using your own ideas and the information in this chapter, choose a topic related to an endangered animal, such as the wolves, somewhere in the world. Plan to speak for two to three minutes on the topic. Make a short outline of your ideas in note form. Practice your talk a few times before you record. Record your talk on tape or audio CD and give it to your teacher for feedback.

▶ **B** After what happened to Keiko, do you think that Luna could rejoin his pod? What do you think the arguments are for moving Luna? What are the arguments against moving Luna? What should be done in cases like this?

To answer these questions, follow these steps:

▶ **1.** Make a list of the reasons for and against returning Luna to his pod.

2. Get together with a small group of people who share your opinion and complete your list of reasons.

3. Check your list with your teacher and then present your ideas to some classmates who prepared the opposing argument.

4. In your group, try to reach agreement about the decision that should be made.

5. Report your decision to the class. Explain the reasons for the decision.

C Follow-Up Reading Search the Internet to find out what has happened in the case of returning Luna to the wild. Read the latest news reports on this remarkable case and report your findings to others in your class.

Writing

A Topic Writing Write about the problem of returning animals to the wild and some possible solutions to this problem. Use the information from the chapter readings as well as ideas from your own reading. Use examples to help you explain your ideas.

B Reaction Writing What do you think about people's reaction to wild animals that they come in contact with? Can people and wild animals share the same environments? What are some examples of successful co-existence you can think of? What are some problems (for example, bear attacks in Canada, or shark attacks in the waters of the southern United States) that have occurred?

Online Study Center   For additional activities, go to the *Reading Matters* Online Study Center at *college.hmco.com/pic/wholeytwo2e*.

12 Protecting Water Resources

Chapter Openers

Survey

▶ **A** **Listing Ideas** Work with a partner or a small group. Make a list of the top ten reasons why people need to have supplies of fresh water.

Water Needs Survey

1. Water to drink
2. _____
3. _____
4. _____
5. _____
6. _____
7. _____
8. _____
9. _____
10. _____

▶ **B** Decide on the five most important reasons and their order of importance. Discuss your ideas about these questions with a partner or a small group.

1. Where does your water supply come from?
2. Have you ever had to reduce the amount of water you use? When?
3. Do you think we will need to ration (use only a specific amount of) water in the future?
4. Are there places where water has disappeared or been polluted?
5. What can be done to keep water clean?
6. How would your life change if there wasn't enough water?

Opinions

▶ Think about where in the world water is supply a problem. How could water be supplied to these areas?

▶ Give your opinion as to whether each of the following methods is possible or not. Circle *P* (possible) or *I* (impossible). Be prepared to talk about the details of these proposed methods: where, how, when, who, and what.

1. P I Desalination (taking salt out of ocean water or seawater)

2. P I Pumping water out of aquifers (lakes under the ground)

3. P I Importing water from places that have enough of a supply

4. P I   Transporting icebergs from the polar caps

5. P I   Requiring people who use too much water to pay or share with people who have too little of their own

6. P I   Recycling wastewater for needs like watering the garden

Exploring and Understanding Reading

Previewing Graphics

This reading is about possible problems with the world's water supply. There are some charts and diagrams that present information related to the topic in the reading. Their purpose is to help the reader get information visually. Before you begin to read, preview the article by looking at this graphic information. Read the text titles and subtitles and answer the following questions.

1. What kind of information will I get out of this reading?
   a. Factual information
   b. Personal opinion
   c. Stories about people
2. What is the overall topic of this reading?
   a. Possible ways to solve the problem of water shortages in the world
   b. Ways to use water for farming
   c. Why it's not a good idea to use too much groundwater

Skimming

> **Reading Tip**

When you skim a longer reading, **don't stop** at difficult vocabulary. Skip over it and **focus on** the **ideas you understand**. ■

Quickly skim the article and find three possible solutions to water shortages.

1. _____

2. _____

3. _____

Work with a partner to compare your answers.

Global Water Shortages

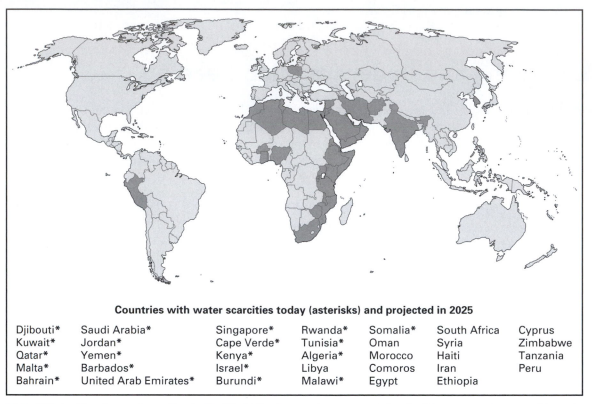

Countries with water scarcities today (asterisks) and projected in 2025

Djibouti*	Saudi Arabia*	Singapore*	Rwanda*	Somalia*	South Africa	Cyprus
Kuwait*	Jordan*	Cape Verde*	Tunisia*	Oman	Syria	Zimbabwe
Qatar*	Yemen*	Kenya*	Algeria*	Morocco	Haiti	Tanzania
Malta*	Barbados*	Israel*	Libya	Comoros	Iran	Peru
Bahrain*	United Arab Emirates*	Burundi*	Malawi*	Egypt	Ethiopia	

Global Water Shortages According to the World Bank, some twenty countries don't have enough renewable water today. By 2025, the situation in these countries will be worse and fourteen other countries will have water supply problems.

Note: Countries that have less than 1,000 cubic meters of water per capita per year fall into the category "water scarce." Water that comes from rain or rivers is called renewable water.

Will the Earth run out of fresh water?

❶   There are 335 million cubic miles of water on Earth, enough to cover the United States to a depth of 93 miles. The problem is that almost 98 percent of it is salt water—unfit to drink or to use for most other human needs, such as agriculture and industry. Only about 2.5 percent of the Earth's water is fresh and almost 99 percent of that small amount is locked up in the form of glaciers and permanent snow cover in the polar regions, or in largely unrenewable underground aquifers. Some groundwater sources can be tapped, but most of the water they contain is nonrenewable, a finite resource just like oil. After it's pumped out of the ground, it's gone forever. In the final analysis, less than 1 percent of the Earth's fresh water is renewable. This is the water found in freshwater lakes and rivers. They are replenished by rainfall, river flow, and springs.

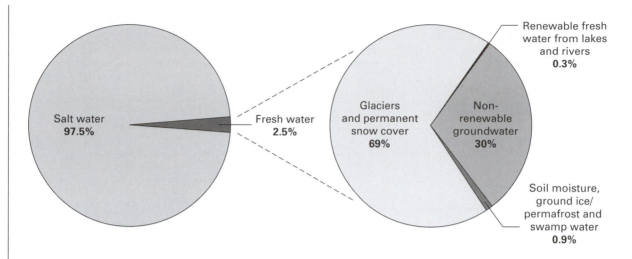

How much water can we use? … Not that much! Seventy-five percent of the Earth is water, but we can use only about 2.5 percent. This small amount is fresh water. But 1.5 percent of the Earth's fresh water is frozen in glaciers or snow, or in non-renewable lakes underground. Only 1 percent of the Earth's water is renewable.

Can technology provide the solution to water shortages?

❷　Given the globe's limitless quantity of salt water, desalination would seem to offer the greatest technological solution to water scarcity. But removing the salt from sea and ocean water has several drawbacks. To begin with, not all water-scarce countries have access to seawater. More importantly, the high cost of desalination makes it infeasible for many developing countries, which are the most seriously affected by water shortages. Most of the world's 7,500 desalination plants are in the Persian Gulf countries with access to the cheap oil supplies required to run them.

❸　Some scientists see solar energy as an alternative to fossil fuels. A solar-powered desalination plant near the Red Sea port of Massawa, Ethiopia, provides enough fresh water for 500 people. But solar power is not feasible in many water-scarce countries. Many proposals focus on transporting water. Some needy regions already rely heavily on water imports. The Balearic Islands of Spain, for example, receive fresh water shipped in from Scotland, while Malta is almost entirely dependent on imported water. But shipping water is only feasible in countries with relatively strong economies. Malta's highly developed tourist trade, for example, generates enough revenue to pay for the water and food it must import.

❹　More inventive proposals to transport water on a larger scale include hauling it in huge plastic bags or towing mammoth chunks of icebergs from polar regions to the Middle East and other needy areas. "The problem is, a lot would disappear on the way through warmer waters," says the World Bank's G. Le Moigne. "Also, you would have to be able to stock the transported water somewhere. So there are ideas galore, but so far we do not have one that is sufficiently affordable."

Country	Percentage of renewable water supplies originating outside borders	Years required for population to double*
Egypt	97	30.1
Netherlands	89	138.6
Cambodia	82	27.7
Syria	79	18.2
Sudan	77	22.4
Iraq	66	18.7
*Excludes migration		

As populations increase, what will countries that get their water from sources outside their borders do? Here are six countries that get more than 50 percent of their renewable water from rivers that are in other countries.

Source: Data from "Sustaining Water: Population and the Future of Renewable Water Supplies," Population Action International, *1993; Peter H. Gleick, ed.,* Water in Crisis: A Guide to the World's Fresh Water Resources, *1993.*

Should water be treated as a marketable commodity?

❺   Historically, water has been treated as a free resource, almost like the air we breathe. But as growing consumption depletes renewable supplies in many parts of the world, water is assuming greater economic value. Water resource managers point repeatedly to California's recent success in promoting conservation by all water consumers and encouraging farmers to sell their surplus water rights to cities. California's Central Basin district, for example, uses wastewater that has gone through three treatment cycles for a number of non-drinking water uses, including irrigation of parks, golf courses, and freeway landscaping. The district also distributes recycled water for use in cooling towers and boilers and certain water-intensive industries such as the manufacturing of carpets and concrete. According to district general manager Mr. Atwater, it is the largest water-recycling project in the United States and a model for new recycling efforts in the United States. "Because of the cost of water and our past droughts, industry and other large customers have tried to become much more efficient in using water and recycling waste streams," he says. "We recycle about 100 million gallons a day. It's like freeing up drinking water for a million people, so we're saving a lot of water."

Scanning

▶ **A** Read the following questions and quickly check to find the answers. Underline the words in the reading that support your answer.

1. How much of Earth's water is fresh water?

   _____

2. Where is most of the fresh water located?

   _____

3. What percent of Earth's water is renewable?

   _____

4. Where does renewable water come from?

   _____

5. Where are most of the world's desalination plants located?

   _____

6. What two areas in the world depend on imported water?

   a. _____

   b. _____

7. Why is transporting icebergs to the Middle East not a good idea?

   _____

8. What does the Central Basin district in California use its wastewater for?

   a. _____

   b. _____

   c. _____

9. How much water does the district recycle daily?

   _____

▶ **B** Circle the correct choice in each sentence. Then, scan the reading to check your answers. Underline the sentence that contains the correct answer.

1. Salt water is **fit / unfit** to drink.

2. Most sources of groundwater are **renewable / nonrenewable**.

3. The high cost of desalination makes it **feasible / infeasible** for many developing countries.

4. Solar power is **feasible / infeasible** in many water-scarce countries.

5. Many proposals for transporting water are **affordable / unaffordable**.

6. California uses wastewater for **drinking / non-drinking** purposes.

7. Something must be done to **encourage / discourage** greater water conservation.

▶ Work with a partner to compare your answers.

Note Taking

▶ **Advantages and Disadvantages** This reading analyzes the advantages and difficulties of different solutions to the problem of water supply. Noting the facts of these ideas helps you to become a critical reader. List three different solutions and the advantages and disadvantages of each in note form.

Solution	Advantage	Disadvantage
1. _____	_____	_____
_____	_____	_____
_____	_____	_____
_____	_____	_____
2. _____	_____	_____
_____	_____	_____
_____	_____	_____
_____	_____	_____
3. _____	_____	_____
_____	_____	_____
_____	_____	_____
_____	_____	_____

▶ Work with a partner. Take turns explaining the information about each of the solutions to each other.

Agree or Disagree

▷ Circle *A* if you agree or *D* if you disagree with the following statements. Compare your ideas with a partner. Be ready to explain the reasons for your choices.

1. A   D   Water should be shared among all countries.

2. A   D   We must reduce the amount of water we waste.

3. A   D   In the future water will be more expensive.

4. A   D   In the future we will have to recycle water more than we do now.

5. A   D   We will need to find new sources of water in the future.

6. A   D   We will need to develop new technology to keep water clean.

▷ Report on one of the statements you agree with to the class.

Applying the Information

▷ **Identifying a Plan** In the first reading of this chapter, there are some suggestions for ways to save water. Quickly read the short article that follows and identify the type of water saving plan that is explained. Circle the correct answer below.

This article is about a

a. plan to transport water.

b. plan to desalinate water.

c. plan to recycle wastewater.

The Living Machine

Dr. Jack Todd is a Canadian marine biologist who is very interested in clean water. He is also interested in saving money, so it's only natural that he is the developer of a small and affordable system to clean wastewater on a very local scale. His "Living Machine" can clean wastewater in your home or in your business.

The "Living Machine" is a system for cleaning wastewater that comes from toilets, baths, dishwashers, washing machines, and any other home plumbing system. The wastewater goes into a big plastic tank where bacteria start to break down the waste. A few days later, after it's processed, the water is brought into a greenhouse filled with plants, fish, and algae who feed on it. With the help of sunlight, the plants and animals remove more chemicals from the water, making it cleaner. Then the water can be reused for washing, flushing toilets, or bathing. It cannot be used for drinking or cooking, but the water is clean enough for watering the lawn, washing the dog, or even for bathing or swimming.

The advantage of this technology is that it is affordable and good for the environment. It costs the same as a commercial septic system. The local government saves tax money it would spend to transport waste to large recycling plants. It is beneficial for the environment because wastewater is not put into the fresh-water supply system. If enough homes and businesses used "Living Machines," it could help to reduce the amount of fresh water we need to take from lakes and rivers, and it could help keep the water supply unpolluted.

Understanding an Extended Example

▶ The preceding reading describes and explains one way to conserve water. It is an "extended" example; in other words, there is a lot of detail about this system. Answer the following questions that focus on the details of this example.

1. What did Jack Todd develop?

   _____

2. What kinds of wastewater can his system clean?

   _____

3. Where is the wastewater cleaned?

   a. _____

   b. _____

4. How are chemicals removed from the water?

   _____

5. a. What can the water be reused for?

   _____

   b. What can't the water be reused for?

   _____

6. What facts show that the system is affordable?

   _____

7. What facts show that the system is good for the environment?

   _____

▶ Compare answers with your partner. Try to agree on the same answers. Check the reading to confirm your answers.

Vocabulary Building

Word Form and Meaning

▶ **A** Match the words in Column A with their meanings in Column B.

Column A

_____ 1. analyze

_____ 2. access

_____ 3. consume

_____ 4. generate

_____ 5. require

Column B

a. to use up or completely finish something

b. to demand or need something

c. to find and make available (data) from a computer

d. to examine something in detail

e. to produce something

▶ **B** Study these five words and their forms: verb, noun, adjective, and adverb. Then choose the correct form for each part of speech in the chart below. These words are commonly found in general and academic texts.

analyze (v.)	access (v.)	consume (v.)	generate (v.)	require (v.)
analysis (n.)	access	consumer	generation	required
analyst (n.)	accessible	consuming	generational	requiring
analyzed (adj.)	accessibility	consumption	generator	requirement
analyzing (adj.)	accessibly	consumed	generating	

Verb	Noun	Adjective	Adverb
access	1. 2.	1.	1.
consume	1. 2.	1. 2.	
generate	1. 2.	1. 2.	
require	1.	1. 2.	

▶ Compare lists with a partner. Try to agree on the same answers.

▶ **C** Write three or more sentences using words from the list.

▶ **D** In English, one of the ways the form of a word can be changed is to add a special suffix, or word ending, to change a verb into a noun. In the following sentences the suffix *-tion*, *-ion*, or *-sion* can be added to a verb root to form nouns.

▶ Choose the correct word to complete the sentences.

1. conserve / conservation

   a. It's important to _____ water for future generations.

   b. The _____ of the country's water supply is important to all of us.

2. solve / solution

   a. They needed to _____ the problems of water supply.

   b. They needed to find a _____ to the problems of water supply.

3. pollute / pollution

   a. Scientists thought that chemical _____ was causing the damage.

   b. If the chemicals _____ the water, the fish may be harmed.

4. desalinate / desalination

   a. They are convinced it's important to _____ the seawater.

   b. They are convinced that the _____ of the seawater is important.

5. reduce / reduction

   a. They decided to _____ the amount of water they were using.

   b. We asked them to make a _____ in the amount of water they use.

6. irrigate / irrigation

   a. The local government wants to use recycled water to _____ the parks and golf courses.

   b. The local government wants to use recycled water for the _____ of parks and golf courses.

▶ Check your answers. Work with a partner and take turns reading your sentences.

▶ **E Synonyms** Match the words in Column A with words that have the same meaning in Column B.

Column A

_____ 1. access

_____ 2. agriculture

_____ 3. drawback

_____ 4. import

_____ 5. mammoth

_____ 6. manufacture

_____ 7. proposal

_____ 8. replenish

_____ 9. required

_____10. unfit

Column B

a. produce

b. disadvantage

c. huge

d. needed

e. fill up again

f. not usable

g. farming

h. plan

i. bring into the country

j. opening

▶ **F Words with the Prefix _re-_** In English some word prefixes have usual meanings. The prefix _re-_ usually means "again," as in the word "renew," or "make it new again."

▶ Give your own definition of the following words. Look at the way the word is used in the reading before you write your definition.

1. renewable _____

2. replenish _____

3. remove _____

4. recycle _____

Vocabulary in Context

▶ You can understand the meaning of a new word by using the words you know to help you make a good guess. Circle the words that help you to guess the meaning of the word in boldface. Write your definition of the word. Then consult a dictionary to check your definition.

1. Because the water was **unfit** to drink, they had to bring in bottled water from the next town. _____

2. They couldn't use the water, because it was **locked up** in the form of glaciers. _____

3. The water is non-renewable, a **finite** resource like oil that is gone forever once it is used. _____

4. Not all countries can get water from **desalination**, because many don't have access to seawater. _____

5. Some needy regions don't have enough water and **rely** on water imports.

_____

6. Malta's highly developed tourist trade generates enough **revenue** to pay for water and food. _____

7. The problem is you would have to **stock** the water somewhere for it to be used. _____

8. They use the recycled water for a number of non-drinking uses such as the **irrigation** of parks. _____

▶ Work with a partner and take turns reading your sentences and giving your definitions.

⦿Expanding Your Language

Reading

This reading expands on the idea of conserving water resources. Notice how much easier it is to understand this now that you have done some reading beforehand.

▶ First, read the following questions. After reading, answer them based on the information in the text.

1. What kind of pollution has been affecting the Alexander River?
2. Where does the pollution come from?
3. How is the pollution being removed?
4. What has been done to restore the river ecosystem?
5. What proof is there that the river is becoming cleaner?
6. How has the work of this project been recognized?
7. Why is this project important?

Coming Together to Save a River

The Alexander River flows through Jewish and Palestinian towns in the middle of Israel, not far from the Mediterranean Sea. It is twenty miles long and, until recently, was extremely polluted. It carried industrial, agricultural, and human waste. Now it is being restored to health. The project is the result of two peoples, Israelis and Palestinians, working together. On the local level, people see that they need to have clean water. Water is important for everyone's survival. The main work of the project is a complex of reservoirs and treatment plants that cost $4 million. The wastes from towns in the West Bank and from seventy other sources of pollution are cleaned in the treatment plants.

The Alexander River has been in bad shape for many years. The river banks had collapsed and the water was not flowing freely. The two peoples cooperated to rebuild the banks. New bushes and trees have been planted to improve the environment. The river has become so clean that the rare Nile soft-shelled turtle is coming back to the area. There are about 70–100 adult turtles living there. Schoolchildren come to the water to learn about these animals that grow as long as three feet and were shown in ancient Egyptian artwork.

The project has only just begun. There is more work to do to continue the cleanup. But the project shows what two communities can do to work together for the good of the environment and each other. In 2003, the project received the top prize in an international restoration competition held in Australia. This year a small group of people involved in the cleanup traveled to the small West African country of Burkina Faso to help that country begin a similar project. Says one man, "Ecology knows no borders … a river can be a bridge between people."

Speaking

▶ **A Oral Presentation** Choose an area of the world and talk about the water resources in that area. Include facts that describe where the water supply comes from, how it is used, what it is used for, and future water problems and possible solutions. Give as many examples as possible.

▶ **B Discussion** Form a group with some classmates who are from different countries. Write three questions to find out about the problems and solutions of water supply. Use your questions to have a discussion about water supply in different parts of the world.

Writing

▶ **A Topic Writing** Write about the problem of water supply and some possible solutions to this problem. Use the information from the chapter reading. Use examples to help you explain your ideas.

▶ **B Reaction Writing** What can governments and citizens do to save water? Write some details about the suggestions you would make. For example, explain what decisions or plans the government should make, how the plans would work, who would be involved, and how they would be paid for.

▶Read On: Taking It Further

Reading Journal

Don't forget to write your **reading journal** and **vocabulary log** entries in your notebook. ▪

▶ There are some very interesting stories that have been written about wild animals and people's relationships with wild animals. One of these stories is *The Call of the Wild*, by the American writer Jack London. You can find this and other stories in condensed or adapted versions. With your teacher's guidance, choose this or another story to read and report on.

Newspaper Articles

▶ Check the paper over a few days and find an interesting article about some aspect of the environment. You could look for an article about animals, forests, or parks, or about an issue like water, land, or air conservation. Prepare to present the information to a partner or a small group.

To prepare, follow these steps:

▶ **1. Skimming** Quickly read the article to get the general idea and to check if the information is interesting.

2. Ask these questions: What are the facts? Who is involved? When? Where? Why? and How?

3. Highlight the important facts. Make notes if it will help you to explain more easily.

4. Practice your presentation.

5. Present your information.

Word Play

▶ Choose ten new words that you would like to learn from the readings in the unit. Try to choose words that are important, such as nouns, adjectives, verbs, or adverbs. Write a sentence using one of the words. Make your own definition of the word. Find a word or phrase that has the same meaning. Check the work with your teacher.

▶ Work with a partner. Tell your partner the definition and the synonym and ask your partner to guess the word. Give one letter of the word's spelling until your partner makes a correct guess.

 **Online Study Center**   For additional activities, go to the **Reading Matters** Online Study Center at *college.hmco.com/pic/wholeytwo2e*.

UNIT 5

Personality

A person is as happy as he makes up his mind to be.

—*Abraham Lincoln*

Introducing the Topic

In this unit you will read about different aspects of human personality. Each of us has our own unique personality. What we call "personality" is the combination of so many different traits; some we are born with and some develop out of life experience. What are some of the ways that we look at an individual's personality? Chapter 13 is about the topic of friendship. How do friendships affect our lives? Chapter 14 explores the feelings of shyness and worry. How do these emotions influence our lives? In Chapter 15 you will discover what some people say our handwriting reveals about our personalities.

▶Points of Interest

Describing Emotions

▶ **A** Look at the following illustration and circle the faces that show how you are feeling right now.

Anxious	Arrogant	Bored	Confident	Curious
Disapproving	Frightened	Happy	Hurt	Indifferent
Innocent	Interested	Joyful	Lonely	Lovestruck
Miserable	Negative	Optimistic	Pained	Regretful
Relieved	Sad	Satisfied	Sexy	Thoughtful

B Put a check (✔) on the illustration next to the following:

1. Three negative emotions
2. Three positive emotions
3. Three emotions that describe your own personality

Discuss your ideas with a partner or a small group.

Discussion Questions

Think about the following questions. Share your ideas with a partner or a small group. Explain your ideas as completely as possible.

1. What is your definition of "personality"?
2. Does an individual's personality change? If so, how and why does it change?
3. What are a few ways that we can find out what someone's personality is like (for example: daily life experiences, personality tests, etc.)?
4. Does our personality influence our lives? How does this happen?

13 The Importance of Friendship

Chapter Openers

What's Your Opinion?

▶ **Agree or Disagree** Circle *A* if you agree or *D* if you disagree with the statement.

1. A D   People of different ages or different backgrounds can never be friends.

2. A D   It takes a long time to know if someone is your friend.

3. A D   We can have friends with very different personalities.

4. A D   Friends have little influence on our lives.

▶ Work with a partner or a small group. Compare your ideas. Explain your ideas with reasons and examples.

Expressions

▶ Here are some expressions about friends and friendship. Discuss what each means with a partner or a small group. Try to agree on a meaning.

1. A friend in need is a friend indeed.
2. Friends do not lose their flavor.
3. Friendship—one heart in two bodies.
4. Your greatest security lies in your friendships.
5. There is no greater enemy than a false friend.

▶ What sayings about friends do you know? Think of one to share with your classmates.

Exploring and Understanding Reading

Predicting

▶ This reading is from a weekly news magazine that gives information about important people and ideas as well as important news of the week. What kind of information do you expect to find in a weekly news magazine article about people's lives? In the following list, check (✔) the item(s) you expect to find.

_____ Who is involved in the story

_____ Where and when the story took place

_____ Long explanations about what happened in the story

_____ Short explanations about what happened in the story

_____ Reasons why the story is important

▶ Compare choices with a partner.

Previewing

▶ Look at the picture, title, and subtitle of this article. Using your predictions and your previewing, make a list of four ideas you expect to find in the reading.

1. _____

2. _____

3. _____

4. _____

▶ Share your ideas with a partner or with a small group.

With a Little Help from Her Friends
Soo Yeun Kim and the Students of Jericho High School

Soo Yeun Kim was the kind of student who shows up in the "most likely to succeed" category in high school yearbooks. At Jericho High School in Jericho, N.Y., the seventeen-year-old was an accomplished flutist, editor of the literary magazine, and a star science student. The week after Thanksgiving, as she was putting the finishing touches on her project for the famous Westinghouse Science Talent Search, she and her close friend Joseph Ching were killed in a car accident on a rain-soaked road just a mile from her home.

Jericho had lost two of its best and brightest students—but their grieving friends refused to let Soo Yeun's hard work go to waste. With only two days before the deadline, a group of her classmates made a commiment to work together and finish her Westinghouse application, some putting off their own work to finish their friend's. Most of her project, a two-year study of bone fragments as they related to the behavior of the Neanderthal man, was already complete. But an eight-page entry form remained, and there were questions that needed answers. What awards had she won? What clubs did she belong to? One question, especially, brought tears to the eyes of her friends: "What would you really like to be doing ten or fifteen years from now?"

The group finished the project in time and, with the assistance of Soo Yeun's science teacher, Allen Sachs (at right in beard and tie), sent it off to Westinghouse with a note explaining what had been done. But the note was torn off, and the judges had no knowledge of the circumstances surrounding Soo Yeun's application. Two months later, her project was selected as one of 40 finalists from more than 1,600 applicants. (Because finalists must be interviewed, Soo Yeun's project could go no further.) It was the first time in the competition's fifty-four-year history that Westinghouse had made an award posthumously—a tribute not only to Soo Yeun Kim's hard work but to her selfless friends as well.

Skimming

▶ Read the complete article quickly and add to or change your prediction statements, then answer the following questions.

1. What happened to Soo Yeun?

   _____

2. What did Soo Yeun's friends do for her?

   _____

Chronology

▶ **Following the Story** Read the following statements. Number each according to its order in the story.

_____ a. Soo Yeun and her close friend were killed in a car accident.

_____ b. Westinghouse gave an award to Soo Yeun.

_____ c. Soo Yeun had worked for two years on a project for the Westinghouse Science Talent Search.

_____ d. Soo Yeun was a star science student.

_____ e. Soo Yeun's friends sent her application along with a note.

_____ f. Soo Yeun's project was selected by the judges.

_____ g. Soo Yeun's friends and teacher filled out her application.

_____ h. A group of Soo Yeun's friends decided to finish her application.

▶ Work with a partner to compare the order of the sentences. Locate and underline the information in the article that matches the statements.

Understanding Descriptive Details

▶ Answer these questions. Underline the details in the reading that support your answer.

1. How did people describe Soo Yeun?

_____

2. How did the writer describe Joseph Ching?

_____

3. What was Soo Yeun's project?

_____

4. What questions were on the application?

_____

5. What happened to the note that was sent?

_____

6. How are Soo Yeun's friends described?

_____

▶ Work with a partner to ask and answer the questions. Look back at the article to compare the information you underlined.

Reacting to the Story

▶ Retell the story of Soo Yeun and her friends and then share your ideas about these questions.

1. What does this story tell us about the power of friendship?
2. Why does the writer call Soo Yeun's friends "selfless"? Do you know of any other examples of selfless friendship?
3. How does society recognize acts of selflessness? Explain with as many examples as you can.

Applying the Information

▶ **Similarities and Differences** Read the following newspaper article. Answer these questions:

1. Did Carol Fleck have selfless reasons to help Ken Purves?
2. Did he accept her offer immediately? Why or why not?
3. How did their friendship develop?
4. What is the negative side of this story? What is the positive side?

New Kidney Is Gift from the Heart

Kelowna, B.C.—Being a perfect match has taken on a whole new meaning to a Kelowna couple married over the weekend. Just a few weeks after their trip down the aisle, Carol Fleck, 48, and Ken Purves, 53, will make a trip into the operating room where Fleck will donate one of her kidneys to her new husband.

"I'll be fine with one kidney," Fleck says. "And I couldn't be giving a kidney up for a man any more full of integrity and character than Ken."

But Fleck didn't decide to give up one of her organs because she was in love. Love actually came later in the equation. The pair had been casual friends at church. When she learned Purves needed a kidney transplant, Fleck decided she would donate one of her healthy organs if she was a match. He was totally surprised by the offer.

"I didn't know how to respond," said Purves, who's been a widower for four years. "I'd been sick for a long time and I'd been on the donor list for more than eighteen months, so I really wasn't talking about it. After all, you really can't go shopping for a kidney."

He eventually accepted Fleck's offer. But she still needed to be tested to see if she was a match.

"I had the tests done, and it takes six weeks to get the results back," said Fleck, a divorcee of eight years. "Ken and I started spending more time together during that six weeks, and the sparks were beginning to fly. By the time we got the results on December 17 that I'd be a good match, the romance was well under way."

On Valentine's Day, Purves asked Fleck to marry him. "I didn't mean for us to get married until after the transplant and we were both healthy," he said. "But Carol suggested we get married beforehand so we could go through it as a married couple."

Their involvement with one another can only help: doctors say transplants work better when there's an emotional attachment between donor and recipient.

After the April 27 operation, the couple will recover together at a Vancouver hospital.

⟩Vocabulary Building

Word Form and Meaning

▶ **A** Match the words in Column A with their meanings in Column B.

Column A

_____ 1. assist

_____ 2. attach

_____ 3. commit

_____ 4. equate

_____ 5. transplant

Column B

a. to move someone or something to a new location

b. to promise to give your attention or time to someone or something

c. to connect or join someone or something to another

d. to help someone

e. to match or put things on the same level

▶ **B** Study these five words and their forms: verb, noun, adjective, and adverb. Then choose the correct form for each part of speech in the chart below. These words are commonly found in general and academic texts.

assist (v.)   attach (v.)   commit (v.)   equate (v.)   transplant (v.)
assist (n.)   attachment   commitment   equated   transplant
assistance (n.)   attached   committed   equation   transplanting
assistant (n.)   attachable   committee   equational   transplantation
assistant (adj.)   equationally   transplanted
assisting (adj)

Verb	Noun	Adjective	Adverb
attach	1.	1.	
		2.	
commit	1.	1.	
	2.		
equate	1.	1.	1.
		2.	
transplant	1.	1.	
	2.		
	3.		

▶ Compare lists with a partner. Try to agree on the same answers.

▶ **C** Write three or more sentences using words from the list.

▶ **D** Many words have more than one meaning. Look at these definitions for the word *assist*.

a. **assist (noun):** a pass made to another player on a team

b. **assist (noun):** a mechanical device that helps in the performance of an act

c. **assist (verb):** to help or give support

d. **assist (verb):** to be present at the performance of some activity

▶ Read the sentences below and write the letter of the correct meaning on the line provided.

1. _____ The **assist** came in the middle of the second period of play.

2. _____ She asked if they could **assist** the students so that the project would be completed on time.

3. _____ It would be hard to **assist** at the birth when she was so far away.

4. _____ He attached an **assist** to the main motor as a back up in case of a failure.

5. _____ She agreed that the **assist** should be credited to another player who had touched the ball after she had.

Vocabulary in Context

▶ **A Jigsaw Sentences** Match the beginning of the sentence in Column A with the best completion of the sentence in Column B.

Column A

_____ 1. When she first learned he needed a transplant,

_____ 2. By the time they got the results,

_____ 3. Doctors say that transplants work better

_____ 4. He'd been on the donor list for a long time

Column B

a. when donor and recipient are emotionally attached.

b. she immediately decided to donate one of her organs.

c. so he had stopped talking about it to everyone.

d. the romance was already underway.

▶ **B** Can the order of these sentences be changed? Write the sentences in reversed clause order below.

1. _____

2. _____

3. _____

4. _____

▶ **C Phrases** Circle the phrase that is closest in meaning to the words in boldface in these sentences. Underline the words in the reading that support your answer.

1. Her grieving friends refused to let Soo Yeun's hard work **go to waste**.
   a. be thrown out
   b. be left over
   c. be used up

2. One question **brought tears to their eyes**.
   a. made them sad
   b. bothered their eyes
   c. made them angry

3. The note was **torn off** and they didn't know about the circumstances of the application.
   a. cut into many pieces
   b. returned
   c. removed

4. They **sent it off** with a note to explain what they had done.
   a. mailed it
   b. exploded it
   c. finished it

5. They **had no inkling** of what had happened.
   a. didn't understand
   b. didn't write
   c. didn't know

6. Carol and Ken will **take a trip down the aisle** together.
   a. take a vacation
   b. go shopping
   c. get married

▶ Check your answers with a partner.

Expanding Your Language

Reading   ▷ Before reading the following selection, read the following questions. After reading, answer them based on the information in the text.

1. Describe what Paul Newman and A. E. Hotchner have created together and its purpose.
2. How long have these two men been friends?
3. What is their friendship like?
4. What problems about the business worried Hotchner?
5. What do the two men credit as the reason for its success?
6. What shows the depth of the two men's friendship? Why is this so surprising?

Newman's Own: Friendship and Business Can Mix

Paul Newman is a well-known American actor. A. E. Hotchner, a successful writer, is not as well known. But the two men are the driving force behind the name brand "Newman's Own." The company that they started produces a line of food products with items such as popcorn, lemonade, spaghetti sauce, and salad dressing. The profits from the sales of these foods go to charity. Over the more than twenty years their company has been in business, it has generated more than $150 million. That money is used to help run camps for terminally-ill children around the world as well as other worthy activities.

Newman and Hotchner are both senior citizens. They've known each other for almost half a century. That's when they both bought houses in the same neighborhood in Connecticut and, consequently, became friends. The quality that describes their friendship best would be: complaining. It seems that these two business partners can never see things the same way. Mr. Hotchner remembers the start of their business adventures together. "He would call me up at all hours of the day and night to ask me about some little detail: could I get him a special type of mustard seed or popcorn." Whenever he'd have a bright idea, says Hotchner, he'd call me to do the research. The business was born in the barn in back of Newman's house. The two men would work together on the recipes and the cooking.

When Hotchner and Newman speak about the success of their business together, they usually talk about its quality, celebrity, and the money that goes to helping others. But there is something else that's there in the mix that they don't talk about. It's their friendship. With all the grumbling about the other person, it isn't always easy to see that the two men are friends. They are. Take Hotchner's critique of Newman's cooking. He doesn't have a lot of praise for his friend's cooking. "Paul's not a great cook, but he knows what he likes." Then he adds one important detail. "If anything happened to me, he's the one I'd go to. And if anything happened to him, I would think he'd come to me."

Speaking

▶ **A Retelling** Choose one of the stories you read in this chapter. Make notes of important facts. Try to include as many of the descriptive details as possible. Prepare three discussion questions about the story. Work with a partner to tell the story and discuss the questions.

▶ **B Two-Minute Taped Talk** Tell a story about an important friendship in your life. Describe some of the events in your friendship. As an example, refer to the first reading in this chapter, and include important details: who, what, where, when, and why. Make a short outline of your ideas in note form. Put the information in chronological order. Practice your talk a few times before you record it.

Writing

▶ **A Topic Writing** Using the notes you wrote for "Speaking," part A, and your discussion with your partner, write about one of the stories you read in this chapter. Write two paragraphs, one about the facts of the story and the other about your reaction to the ideas in the story.

▶ **B Personal Writing** Write about the topic you chose for the "Two-Minute Taped Talk" or about your own ideas on the topic of friendship.

Online Study Center   For additional activities, go to the *Reading Matters* Online Study Center at *college.hmco.com/pic/wholeytwo2e*.

14 Living with Our Emotions

Chapter Openers

Discussion Questions

▶ Think about the following questions. Discuss your ideas with a partner or a small group.

1. Do you think shyness is positive, negative, or both?
2. How do people become shy? Are we born shy, or does experience cause shyness?
3. Can people overcome shyness?
4. Do you think worrying is positive, negative, or both?
5. What things in a person's life is it reasonable to worry about? What is it not reasonable to worry about?
6. Can people learn to stop worrying?

Paired Readings

▶ In this section, you will find two different stories on the same theme. Choose one of the two to work with. Prepare to explain the story to someone who read the same story and then to a person who read the other story.

1 Coping with Shyness

Previewing

▶ Read the title and the first and last sentences of each paragraph. Then circle the best statement of the main topic of this reading.

a. The reasons that some people are shy
b. Shyness: effects, reasons, and some ways to overcome it
c. Our understanding of shyness and how it can affect people's lives

▶ Compare answers with a partner. Then read the entire story quickly. As you read, look for the main ideas in each paragraph of the reading.

Can Shyness Be Overcome?

❶   Shy people don't enjoy being with others. They feel very uncomfortable or embarrassed in any situation where others will notice or pay attention to them. Some people feel shy occasionally, while others feel shy all the time. Some claim that shyness allows them to process more information, to look at things more closely, and to listen more completely. But most people would agree that being shy puts people at a disadvantage. Shy people feel uneasy in social situations. They are often too worried about what other people think of them to be relaxed. At work, they dread having to speak at meetings or interact with their coworkers. Extremely shy people may even experience feelings of loneliness and depression, because their feelings prevent them from making friends, trying new experiences, and achieving important goals in life.

❷   Important research has shown some of the reasons for shyness. Shyness is, to some extent, genetic. This means that some people, about fifteen percent of us, are shy from birth. Even before being born, the hearts of shy children beat much faster than the hearts of other children. As newborns, these babies feel nervous and cry around others. As very young children, they seem afraid of new experiences. They blush and become embarrassed and some even shake with fear when faced with new people and experiences. But that does not mean that all shy babies necessarily become shy adults. Genetic traits can be modified. In fact, most of the children who are born shy lose their shyness over time. Positive experiences help the children to develop their feelings of self-esteem or self-worth. A shy child who is given the chance to develop an ability for music or sports will gain skills and the confidence to overcome shyness. A parent's praise for the child's accomplishments, as well as a tolerance for failure, is important. Unfortunately, however, not all children develop the confidence and experience to overcome their shyness. Some may suffer feelings of nervousness for many years. The good news is that shy adults can learn to overcome their fears.

❸   There are many ways shy adults can gradually gain control of their uncomfortable feelings. First, they can learn ways to introduce themselves and join in a conversation with others. For example, they can learn how to find common ground for conversation by relating shared experiences, or by asking questions to show the speaker they are interested. Second, they can learn how to ask others about themselves. They can have three or four topics of universal interest to pursue, such as the weather, work, school, or the daily news. They can learn some practical speaking techniques. One technique is to write down the questions you want to ask. Plan what to say, then write the dialogue of what to say and practice the beginning lines. Active listening techniques are useful in overcoming shyness, too. Learn to listen carefully to what other people say in the course of informal conversation. A good way to do this is to make a mental note of a person's interests as they come up in conversation. A second technique is to listen to the way people begin or end conversations and choose the lines to use in a similar situation. Finally, relaxation techniques, such as practicing slow breathing to calm down and thinking about a positive memory, are useful ways to reduce the fear of contact with others. These techniques help a shy person stay calm, look others in the eye, listen, and keep talking.

Main Ideas of Paragraphs

▶ Write the number of the paragraph that best fits each of the following main ideas.

a. _____ How adults can overcome shyness

b. _____ How being shy affects people

c. _____ Our understanding of the causes of shyness

▶ Compare answers with a partner.

Note Taking

Reading Tip

Analyzing information to see the difference between **general** (sub-points) and **specific** information (the details) is an important critical reading skill. ■

▶ **Recognizing Supporting Points and Details** Reread the paragraph about the causes of shyness (2) and the paragraph about what to do to overcome shyness (3). Underline the important facts in these paragraphs. From the information you underlined, make notes of the details for each of the sub-points in these paragraphs. Remember to write key words and phrases only. Do not write complete sentences. Be sure you understand the ideas and can explain them to others.

Main Ideas	Supporting Points/Details
2. Different causes of shyness	1. Genetic cause of shyness
	2. Influences from experience

3. Techniques to overcome
   shyness in adults

1. Ways to introduce themselves
   and join in conversation

2. Techniques for speaking to others

3. Techniques for listening to others

4. Relaxation techniques

▶ Work with a partner and take turns comparing the details you wrote. If necessary, look back at the information to add any facts you didn't note or correct any facts you need to.

Answering Questions from Notes

▶ Use your notes to answer these questions. Circle *T* for true and *F* for false. If the statement is false, give the correct information.

1. T F   A majority of people are shy from birth.

2. T F   Shy children will remain shy throughout their life.

3. T F   Some experiences help people to gain skills and the confidence to overcome shyness.

4. T F   Shy people can learn to start conversations.

5. T F   Shy people do not need to learn to listen.

6. T F   Relaxation techniques are effective ways to control negative feelings.

Interviewing

▶ Answer the questionnaire on the topic you read about. Add questions based on the reading or on your own ideas. Interview two people who read the same information. Write their answers in note form on a separate page.

Questionnaire: Shyness

You: _____   Student A: _____   Student B: _____

1. Do you think you are a shy person?
   a. Yes   b. No   c. Sometimes
2. If you answered no, have you ever felt shy in the past?
3. What experiences do people feel shy about?
   a. Talking to someone you like
   b. Talking to someone you want to like you
   c. Talking to someone older than you
   d. Talking to a person of the opposite sex
   e. Talking to a member of your family
   f. Talking to authorities (teachers, bosses, doctors, etc.)
   g. Meeting people one-to-one
   h. Meeting people in a group
4. Check the ways to overcome shyness that you think are effective.
   a. Try to speak to someone every day.
   b. Join an activity you like.
   c. Listen to how others begin conversations.
   d. Practice having a conversation.
   e. Talk to a counselor about your problems.

Making a Chart to Show Results

▷ Work with a partner or with others who answered the same questionnaire as you. Make a list of the results from all the questionnaires in the following chart in note form. Try to summarize the results for your report. For example, you can note the total number who responded yes, who responded no, or who gave similar answers to a question.

Title of Questionnaire: _____			
Question 1	**Question 2**	**Question 3**	**Question 4**

②Coping with Worry

Previewing

▶ Read the title and the first and last sentences of each paragraph. Then circle the best statement of the main topic of this reading.

a. The ways that worry affects people's lives

b. The ways to cope with worrying

c. Understanding the different effects of worrying on people's lives and how people can learn to cope

▶ Compare answers with a partner. Then read the entire story quickly. As you read, look for the main ideas in each paragraph of the reading.

Don't Let Your Worries Get to You

❶   Everyone worries at one time or another. It is a part of our everyday lives. We worry about deadlines, about financial problems, about our relationships with others. Surprisingly, the fact is that worrying is not always a bad thing. Some amount of worry is necessary because it gives us time to concentrate on a problem and find possible solutions or ways to deal with it. Some worry is stimulating. It can propel you to do better work or to complete work on time. When you worry about a problem, you feel uncomfortable. If you don't want to feel uncomfortable, then you will take action to correct the problem. But in other cases, our worries can interfere with our problem-solving abilities. We worry so much that it stops us from taking the steps needed to solve the problem. If it continues, worrying can take away our energy and lead to physical problems such as fatigue, headaches, muscle pain, and insomnia.

❷   If your worries begin to feel overwhelming, don't despair, because there are ways to lower your "worry level." There are two useful techniques to use. One technique is called "progressive relaxation." Lie on the floor or a flat surface, such as your bed. Then focus on a specific part of your body, such as your neck and shoulders. Tighten that part of your body. When it feels hard and tense, release the tension and relax. Do this for all the major parts of your body. Continue until you feel totally relaxed. Do this once or twice a day for about ten minutes. When your body is relaxed, it is not as easy to feel worried. The second technique is regular meditation. Sit in a quiet place and close your eyes. Repeat a simple sound that you find pleasing. Repeating a sound helps keep out other thoughts. Do this twice a day for twenty minutes. It helps to relax your mind. When you use these two techniques, you help keep your mind and your body from worrying. In addition to techniques that relieve the body and mind of tension, it is important to develop practical problem-solving techniques to resolve the worries. Worriers often spend a lot of unproductive mental energy thinking, "I'll never solve this problem" or "This is just too much for me." Professional counselors or therapists can help worriers to change these negative messages and replace them with more positive thoughts.

❸ Unfortunately, for some individuals, worrying is compulsive. In these cases, people find they cannot stop worrying. The reasons for worry are often unlikely events or ideas that are, in some way, irrational. Yet, even this troubling behavior can be modified, especially with professional help. To help someone who worries constantly or in some irrational way, suggest the following steps. First, help the person become aware of worrying thoughts when they first begin. Recognizing the beginning of a worry cycle is very important. The second step is to learn to recognize how one's body feels when the worrying starts. It is important not to allow a repetitive cycle of worry to set in. Instead, as soon as worrying thoughts appear, the person should ask the following questions: What is the possibility of this problem occurring? Could something other than that happen? Could positive actions be taken if the problem occurs? Most people do not experience these kinds of worries. But when continual worrying becomes a problem, it is good to have some strategies for coping.

Main Ideas of Paragraphs

▶ Write the number of the paragraph that best fits each of the following main ideas.

a. _____ Techniques for coping with compulsive worrying

b. _____ How worrying affects us

c. _____ Some techniques for managing our everyday worries

▶ Compare answers with a partner.

Note Taking

 Recognizing Supporting Points and Details   Reread the paragraph about how worrying affects us (1) and the paragraph about ways to cope with everyday worries (2). Underline the important facts in these paragraphs. From the information you underlined, make notes of the details for each of the sub-points in these paragraphs. Remember to write key words and phrases only. Do not write complete sentences. Be sure you understand the ideas and can explain them to others.

Main Ideas	Supporting Points/Details
1. How worry affects us	1. Everyday worries
	2. Benefits of worrying
	3. Problems with worrying
2. Techniques to cope with everyday worries	1. Technique 1
	2. Technique 2
	3. Problem solving

⏵ Work with a partner and take turns comparing the details you wrote. If necessary, look back at the information to add any facts you didn't note or correct any facts you need to.

Answering Questions from Notes

⏵ Use your notes to answer these questions. Circle *T* for true or *F* for false. If the statement is false, give the correct information.

1.   T   F   Worrying can be beneficial.

2.   T   F   Worries can keep us from solving problems effectively.

3.   T   F   Worrying affects our mind but not our body.

4.   T   F   Meditation helps the body to relax.

5.   T   F   Problem-solving techniques can be learned.

Interviewing   ▶ Answer the questionnaire on the topic you read about. Add questions based on the reading or on your own ideas. Interview two people who read the same information. Write their answers in note form on a separate page.

Questionnaire: Worrying

You: _____   Student A: _____   Student B: _____

1. How often do you worry?
   a. Always   b. Sometimes   c. Never
2. What do you usually worry about?
   a. Everyday problems
   b. Things that are likely to happen
   c. Things that are unlikely to happen
   d. Big decisions that have to be made
   e. Small decisions that have to be made
3. When you are worried, what do you do?
   a. Think about possible solutions
   b. Think about the negative things that will happen
   c. Think about how my worries will affect other people
   d. Ask for advice from friends and family
   e. Ask for expert advice from a counselor or other advisor

Making a Chart to Show Results   ▶ Work with a partner or with others who answered the same questionnaire as you. Make a list of the results from all the questionnaires in the following chart in note form. Try to summarize the results for your report. For example, you can note the total number who responded yes, who responded no, or who gave similar answers to a question.

Title of Questionnaire: _____		
Question 1	**Question 2**	**Question 3**

Comparing the Readings

Discussing the Information

▶ Work with a partner who read a different selection. Use your notes and the results of your questionnaire to explain the information to your partner.

You can begin by **asking** your partner to **answer** the **questionnaire** about your topic before presenting your information. ■

Reacting to the Reading

▶ Using the ideas in the two readings, answer these questions.

1. Do shyness and worrying have similar or different effects on personality?
2. Are the strategies for reducing these problems similar or different?
3. Which problem do you think is more common or more serious? Explain.
4. Do you know any reasons for these problems that are not mentioned in the readings?
5. What other solutions for these problems do you know of?

Vocabulary Building

Word Form and Meaning

▶ **A** Match the words in Column A with their meanings in Column B.

Column A

_____ 1. concentrate

_____ 2. modify

_____ 3. achieve

_____ 4. release

_____ 5. tense

Column B

a. to hold tight or rigid

b. to let go or free oneself of something

c. to pay attention or focus on someone or something

d. to change in some way

e. to do or accomplish something important

B Study these five words and their forms: verb, noun, adjective, and adverb. Then choose the correct form for each part of speech in the chart below. These words are commonly found in general and academic texts.

concentrate (v.)   achieve (v.)   modify (v.)   release (v.)   tense (v.)
concentration (n.)   achiever   modification   release   tensely
concentrate (n.)   achievable   modifier   released   tensing
concentrated (adj.)   achievement   modifiable   tension
concentratedly (adv.)   modifiability   tensed
                                       modified   tenseness

Verb	Noun	Adjective	Adverb
achieve	1.	1.	
	2.		
modify	1.	1.	
	2.	2.	
	3.		
release	1.	1.	
tense	1.	1.	1.
	2.	2.	

Compare lists with a partner. Try to agree on the same answers.

C Write three or more sentences using words from the list.

D Adjectives to Nouns In English, the form of the word can change when it is used as a different part of speech. For example, a suffix (ending) can be added to change the adjective *happy* to the noun *happiness*. Some common noun suffixes include -ness, -ment, and -tion.

Choose the correct form of the word for each of the following sentences. In the parentheses ( ), write which part of speech, noun (n.) or adjective (adj.), is needed to complete the sentence.

1. shy / shyness

   a. People are often _____ (   ) when they meet people for the first time.

   b. Researchers think that _____ (   ) affects a great number of people.

2. relaxed / relaxation

   a. She didn't want to go because she wouldn't feel _____ (   ) talking to so many people.

   b. She decided to go home for a night of _____ (   ).

3. perfect / perfection

   a. Shy people think that they have to be _____ (   ) when they undertake any new project.

   b. It was clear that she expected nothing but _____ (   ) from herself.

4. nervousness / nervous

   a. She kept asking me, "Why do I feel so _____ (   )?"

   b. Her _____ (   ) was very easy to see.

5. lonely / loneliness

   a. After her only daughter moved away, she felt _____ (   ).

   b. The _____ (   ) she felt made all of us very sad.

▶ **E Synonyms** Match the words in Column A with the words in Column B that have a similar meaning.

Column A

_____ 1. calm

_____ 2. productive

_____ 3. fatigue

_____ 4. contact

_____ 5. dread

_____ 6. release

_____ 7. irrational

_____ 8. opportunity

_____ 9. notice

_____ 10. behavior

_____ 11. worry

_____ 12. technique

Column B

a. unreasonable

b. action

c. let go

d. characteristics

e. observe

f. reduce

g. turn red with embarrassment

h. giving good results

i. possibility

j. tiredness

k. procedure

l. meet

_____ 13. traits   m. anxiety

_____ 14. minimize   n. relaxed

_____ 15. blush   o. an extreme fear of

▶ **F Antonyms** The prefix *un-*, meaning "not," is added to the beginning of some words to give that word a negative or opposite meaning, for example, *happy* and *unhappy*.

▶ Scan the readings and find as many words as you can that begin with the prefix *un-*. Write the word and give its antonym. Use the word in a sentence of your own.

Word   **Antonym**

_____   _____

_____   _____

_____   _____

_____   _____

_____

Here are some other negative prefixes:

   il-, as in *legal / illegal*
   in-, as in *adequate / inadequate*
   im-, as in *possible / impossible*

▶ Write a short list of words you know that have antonyms that begin with a negative prefix.

_____   _____

_____   _____

_____   _____

▶ Check your list with your teacher.

Expanding Your Language

Reading

This reading is about the quality of sharing. Notice how much easier it is to understand this now that you have done some reading beforehand.

▶ First, read the questions. After reading, answer them based on the information in the text.

1. What lessons are considered important for children to learn?
2. Are these lessons only important in childhood? Explain.
3. What are some parents doing to encourage their children to learn to share?
4. Why is this important for the family?
5. What other advantages does this sharing bring?
6. What problem do some colleges report about housing?
7. What examples of sharing are found among other mammals?
8. Why do vampire bats share?
9. Why is the possibility that sharing is genetic a comfort to parents?

Sharing

We're taught that it's usually a good thing to share. The lessons are taught early. Every two-year-old in day care is told that they have to share—whether it's the toys they are playing with or that yummy snack they want for themselves. We're taught that teaching children to share is important for their emotional growth—it instills a sense of empathy with others that is one of those crucial markers for success later in life. Now some parents are choosing to have their kids share bedrooms, even when they don't have to. Many parents remember sharing bedrooms with siblings when they were young. They want their children to have that experience.

There are a lot of reasons why sharing a bedroom with a brother or sister could be a good thing. First, it gives the family a better sense of togetherness. In today's world, where kids spend less and less time together with other family members, this could be a good thing. Second, some experts say that children who share a room with a sibling sleep better and that it helps strengthen the child's character. Then, when kids leave to go to college or to live away from home, they are more tolerant and understanding of others and less bothered by the everyday annoyances of living together. Some colleges report that over ninety percent of freshmen have never shared a room and, before the year is over, nearly one-third make a complaint about their roommate with the school.

Although we can learn how to share at home and at school, maybe those are lessons that just come naturally. It's possible that the desire to "do the right thing" is in our genes. Sharing may be innate and one of the keys to survival. Wolves, dogs, monkeys, humans, and vampire bats are mammals that share with others. The case of vampire bats is instructive. They have irregular mealtimes because they can't always find enough willing donors to supply them with their only food—blood. Other members of the colony may be too sick or too busy nursing babies to hunt. But if bats go three days without eating, they will die. They rely on other members of their colony to bring back excess blood for them to eat. It probably makes sense to do this, because any bat could find itself in need of a meal.

If sharing is genetic, then parents can take some comfort in that knowledge and be patient when the arguments over who gets the top bunk bed start to annoy.

Speaking

▷ **Two-Minute Taped Talk** Use the notes and ideas you prepared for the paired reading. Organize your notes to prepare a two-minute talk on the parts of the information you think are important. You can choose to present the information you heard about from your partner, or you can combine parts of both articles in your talk. Make an outline of your ideas in note form. Practice your talk a few times before you record it. Try to explain as clearly and naturally as possible.

Writing

▷ **Topic Writing** Based on your notes for the paired reading and your discussion with your partner, write about the information you read. In separate paragraphs, write about the facts and your reaction to the ideas in the reading.

 *Online Study Center* For additional activities, go to the *Reading Matters* Online Study Center at *college.hmco.com/pic/wholeytwo2e.*

15 Handwriting and Our Personality

Chapter Openers

Discussion Questions

▶ In signing a document, such as a passport or personal check, we write our signature. Write your signature on the following line:

_____

▶ Think about the following questions. Share your ideas with a partner or a small group.

1. Is your signature easy or difficult to read?
2. Do you usually write your signature the same way?
3. Has your signature changed over time? How?
4. How do you feel about your handwriting?
5. Do you find it easy or difficult to read other people's handwriting?
6. What can we learn about people's personalities from analyzing their handwriting?

Free Writing

▶ Free write your ideas in answer to the following questions.

1. Why is handwriting important?
2. Compare your handwriting in your first and second languages. What are the similarities and differences?

**Analyzing
Graphics**

▶ **A Getting Information from Diagrams** Complete either Set A or Set B. Circle your answers.

Set A

1. Who is moodier, A or B?

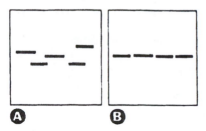

Ⓐ   Ⓑ

2. Who likes to be in the middle of everything?

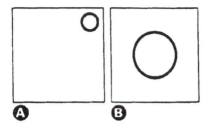

Ⓐ   Ⓑ

3. Who is lying about his or her age?

Ⓐ / am 36 years old.

Ⓑ / am   36 years old

4. Which "Jack" is going to get a raise in his salary?

Figure A

Please have Jack come see me

Figure B

Please have Jack come see me .

▶ Discuss your answers with a partner. Ask your teacher to confirm that you have chosen the correct answers.

Set B

5. Who has a higher IQ?

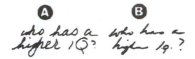

6. Which person is dishonest about money?

7. Which "Mrs. Smith" wants a divorce from "Mr. Smith"?

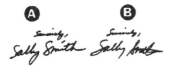

8. Which one of these two writers is more likely to break the law?

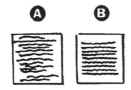

▶ Discuss your answers with a partner. Ask your teacher to confirm that you have chosen the correct answers.

▶ **B** Work with a person who has worked on a different set of diagrams. Ask your partner to answer your set of questions. Discuss the reasons for your choices before giving the answers.

▶Exploring and Understanding Reading

Predicting

▶ This reading is on the topic of graphology, the analysis of handwriting. What ideas do you expect the reading to contain? Check the items you expect to find in the following list.

_____ Origin of handwriting analysis

_____ What handwriting analysis can't tell you

_____ How handwriting analysis works

_____ How handwriting analysis is used

_____ Who doesn't use handwriting analysis

▶ Compare answers with a partner.

Skimming

Remember to **read quickly** when you **skim**. Don't let yourself stop to think about each word individually or about any one word that you may not understand immediately. ▪

▶ Skim the reading and check any of the predictions in the preceding list that you found there. Write three main ideas that you remember from the reading. Share your ideas with a partner. Make a list of common ideas with your classmates.

1. _____

2. _____

3. _____

Graphology: Can It Be Trusted?

❶   Graphology is more than just the study of handwriting. It is the study of all forms of graphic movement, including drawing and doodling. In the United States, graphology has not been considered a legitimate science, but it is studied seriously in Europe, where it developed in the early twentieth century along with the science of psychiatry. Psychiatrists such as Freud and Jung thought this analysis was a very useful tool for understanding both the conscious and the unconscious workings of the mind. For them, handwriting was like a window into the brain. They could look into a person's personality by examining certain movements of the pen, the way the size or style of the handwriting changed, or if an unusual amount of space was left between words in a sentence. Today, graphology firms claim that up to 400 different features of handwriting can reveal the writer's undisclosed, even unconscious, mental states. From a writing sample, graphologists say they can find out the following things about a person:

- Country/region of origin
- Level of intelligence
- Emotional stability
- Aptitudes and talents
- Leadership qualities
- Honesty level
- Physical activity level
- Work/school performance
- Alcoholism or drug abuse

❷   In general, graphologists use five different tools in analyzing written or graphic work. These are:

a. *Physical signs:* When a writer's hand shakes, the writing will shake. When a writer is tense and nervous, the person will push harder on the page. These signs could indicate illness, dishonesty, or drug or alcohol abuse. Or it might be that the person is trying to hide his or her true identity.

b. *Psychological signs:* A graphologist has to understand basic psychological theory. For example, one of Freud's ideas was that if a person overdid something, it meant that the opposite was true. If the word *love* in the sentence "I love you" was written in letters very much larger than the rest, the graphologist would know that, according to Freud's theory, it could mean that the writer does not feel love.

c. *Universal concepts:* According to anthropologist Desmond Morris, there are certain universal body movements showing emotions such as sadness, love, pain, and anger. Because handwriting is one of our body movements, we can assume a link between a movement and an emotion. For example, a person who writes with an upward motion feels happy and a person who writes big feels important.

d. *Common-sense signs:* A person who is neat and tidy will write in an orderly way. People who are messy or don't like their name will not write their signature clearly.

e. *Scientific method:* A lot of research involves the study of large numbers of handwriting samples. Graphologists get writing samples from special groups of people. Then they compare these samples to the handwriting of the general population. For example, in one study, criminals serving time in prison were asked to write on a blank page. Researchers found that many did not begin their sentences at the left-hand margin, a general rule of writing that is learned in school. Through research, graphology has identified twenty-five different handwriting traits that are more common among criminals than in others.

3 Can graphology be trusted to give reliable results? The answer is not clear. But there is growing interest in graphology in the United States. Businesses are beginning to look at handwriting analysis as a way to find the right employee. It is expensive to hire workers, train them, and then six months later find that they are not right for the job. The head of a car dealership is one example of some 6,000 business executives who admit using handwriting analysis to help hire the right people. Tom Payette's car dealership is worth $25 million. With handwriting analysis, he has reduced the rate of employees leaving the job to half of the national average. He also uses handwriting analysis to help decide promotions and other job changes. The results are not 100 percent accurate. But if it saves thousands of dollars in lost time and training, then executives like Tom Payette say it is worth it.

4 There is one area in which handwriting analysis may prove useful and that is the area of medical diagnosis. This finding comes from the work of a team of scientists from the University of Hamburg in Germany. They enlisted the help of volunteers to write while in a brain scanner. From this research they found that the part of the brain closest to the top of the head was one of the main areas responsible for writing. This area is responsible for controlling all kinds of movements. It is not, however, a part of the brain that is associated with personality. But analysis of writing may prove useful in diagnosing illnesses that affect motor coordination. Diseases such as multiple sclerosis, Parkinson's disease, Huntington's, and others are just some of the conditions that can affect handwriting in specific ways. Thus, handwriting analysis could help provide clues as to the location of various disorders in the brain and could even be used in diagnosis. Detecting some changes in handwriting is a very precise way to identify certain neurological conditions.

Scanning for Details

▶ Answer the following questions. Underline the information in the reading that supports your answer.

1. What is graphology and what are the varying opinions about its validity as a science?

_____

2. What three characteristics of handwriting did psychiatrists look at to understand personality?

_____

3. What quantity and kind of information do graphologists say they can find from looking at a person's writing?

_____

▶ Write the answers to question 4 in the chart below.

4. a. What are the five different types of diagnostic tools a graphologist uses?

   b. How is each tool used? What information can you get from using this tool?

Type of Tool	How It Works	Information It Provides
a.		
b.		
c.		
d.		
e.		

5. a. What are businesses interested in using handwriting analysis for?

   _____

   b. Why is handwriting analysis interesting for businesses?

   _____

6. How can handwriting analysis prove useful to medicine? What applications could it have?

   _____

   _____

▶ Work with a partner to compare your answers.

Applying the Information

The next reading is an excerpt from an interview with graphologist Andrea McNicol. Andrea studied graphology at the University of Heidelberg and the Sorbonne. She teaches a course on the subject at the University of California, and she has given expert testimony in several court cases involving handwriting analysis. She is explaining to the interviewer how she used her skills in handwriting analysis to help solve a crime in which money was stolen from a company by an employee.

▶ From the information you have gathered so far, do you think she will show that handwriting analysis:

a. can solve a crime directly?
b. can solve a crime indirectly?
c. cannot solve a crime at all?

▶ Discuss your prediction with a partner. Read the selection as quickly as possible to see if your prediction is correct.

The Lowdown on Handwriting Analysis

Andrea: I've had people make some concerted attempts to mask their writing, but it virtually never works. A lie can be identified on the page. See for yourself. Take a look at the two paragraphs:

> **Cashier A**
>
> I stocked the frozen food section between 4 + 5 a.m. I cashed out registers 3 4 and 5 before leaving and put approximately $2700 into the deposit slot in the safe. I left at 6.
>
> **Janitor**
>
> And there was a pill in the darey ile which I cleaned up. I put away the cart and put the trash in the back, and then I left work at my usual time of 6:00 in the morning.

Andrea: I investigated a case a few years ago involving a theft of $52,000 from the vault of a department store. The theft occurred sometime between 10 P.M. and 6 A.M. Assuming that it was an inside job, because there were no signs of forced entry, the owners asked the two workers on duty that night to write down what their activities were. What stands out in these two letters?

Doris: The cashier's writing seems strained … and the slant is a little inconsistent. The janitor has a variety of slants, too, yet his letter seems less stressed.

Andrea: You're right about the slants. Cashier A may have a tendency to repress, but that doesn't necessarily mean criminal intent. A good first step in interpreting a page is to examine the spacing. If there are exaggerated spaces between words, the writer's mind was pausing or hesitating while writing them. Why were they hesitating? You've got to make an *effort* to lie on the page, an effort that interrupts the normal flow of your writing. The truth usually flows pretty easily.

So what can we conclude from the statements? It seems clear that the large spaces in the janitor's letter between the words *at* and *my* as well as between *of* and *6:00* suggest that he did not leave at the time indicated.

I called the manager and said that I could not conclude from the letters who stole the money, but that the janitor was probably lying about the time at which he'd left that night. It turned out that he was told to leave early by the day manager, who had unexpectedly shown up two hours early that morning, but hadn't informed anyone of his arrival. The manager was later identified as the thief.

Analyzing Information

▶ Work with a partner. Agree on your answers to the following questions. Look back at the reading to confirm your answers.

1. Did handwriting analysis produce direct, indirect, or no evidence of the crime? _____

2. Would you change your predicted answer? _____ Why?

Reacting to the Reading

▶ **Useful or Not?** Referring to the readings in this chapter and your own ideas, answer the following questions.

Do you think that handwriting analysis can be useful in helping people make decisions when they are

- hiring new employees?
- diagnosing emotional problems?
- solving crimes?
- establishing the identity of a person?

◗Vocabulary Building

**Word Form
and Meaning**

◗ **A** Match the words in Column A with their meanings in Column B.

Column A

_____ 1. enforce

_____ 2. detect

_____ 3. identify

_____ 4. indicate

_____ 5. interpret

Column B

a. to explain or translate something

b. to show or point to something

c. to carry out an order to follow a law or rule

d. to find out or notice something

e. to name or know someone or something

◗ **B** Study these five words and their forms: verb, noun, adjective, and adverb. Then choose the correct form for each part of speech in the chart below. These words are commonly found in general and academic texts.

enforce (v.)	detect (v.)	identify (v.)	indicate (v.)	interpret (v.)
enforcement (n.)	detective	identity	indication	interpretation
enforcer (n.)	detectability	identification	indicative	interpretive
enforceability (n.)	detectable	identifying	indicator	interpreter
enforceable (adj.)	detection	identifiable	indicatively	interpretively
	detector	identifiably	indicatory	interpretable

Verb	Noun	Adjective	Adverb
detect	1. 2. 3. 4.	1.	
identify	1. 2.	1. 2.	1.
indicate	1. 2.	1. 2.	1.
interpret	1. 2.	1. 2.	1.

◗ Compare lists with a partner. Try to agree on the same answers.

▶ **C** Write three or more sentences using words from the list.

▶ **D** The suffix *-ist* is added to a noun form to indicate a person who is an expert or a student of a particular field of study or who works in that field. One example is the word *biologist*, meaning "a person who studies or works in biology."

   Scan the reading "Graphology: Can It Be Trusted?" and find examples of nouns ending in *-ist*. Write the noun and give a definition in your own words.

Noun   **Meaning**

_____   _____

_____   _____

_____   _____

▶ **E** Write the adjective form of the following words.

Noun   **Adjective**

1. intelligence   _____

2. space   _____

3. emotion   _____

4. psychology   _____

5. psychiatry   _____

6. criminal   _____

7. importance   _____

▶ Which word has the same form as an adjective and as a noun? _____

▶ **F Antonyms** Use what you know about the prefixes that can mean "not" and scan the readings to find words that have a negative prefix. Write the word and its antonym. Number 1 is given as an example.

1. unconscious   conscious

2. _____   _____

3. _____   _____

4. _____   _____

5. _____   _____

▶ Tell your partner a word, and ask for the correct antonym.

Expanding Your Language

Reading   ▷ Before reading the selection, read the following questions. After reading, answer them based on the information in the text.

1. When do the police use handwriting analysis as a crime investigation tool?
2. What are the three different types of analysts involved in identifying a criminal?
3. Of the three types, which is used when someone has signed a check using another person's name?
4. Of the three types, which can be used to develop a profile of the criminal?
5. How would experts conduct an investigation in cases that use handwriting analysis?

The Letter Detective

When a serious crime has been committed, law enforcement officials will look for clues in a number of different ways. One avenue to explore is handwriting analysis. This is used in cases where a letter or letters are sent by the criminal to the police, the media, or the victims. Some examples of these kinds of cases are that of the Unabomber, serial murderers, and anthrax attacks in the United States. There are three types of handwriting analysts involved in attempts to identify the writer. The first type of handwriting expert is a forensic document examiner. This person analyzes each letter and word and their placement on the page to determine the identity of the writer. This kind of examiner is called on to establish forgery, in cases where documents are changed in some way, or in cases where there is a ransom note. The second type of expert is a forensic linguistics specialist. This person analyzes word choice, phrasing, syntax, and nearly a dozen other language categories to identify the author. An example of this type of work is that of matching the letters of the Unabomber to letters he sent to his family. The third type of expert is a graphologist. This individual applies subjective psychological analysis to handwriting characteristics to look for personality and character traits.

All of these experts would require that a writer or suspected writer make numerous handwritten samples of the questioned text. The text would be read to them, not copied. They would also require a large range of samples of the person's customary writing for comparison.

Speaking

▶ **Oral Presentation** Collect writing samples from one or two people. Based on the information in the readings, analyze the samples. Prepare notes about the findings you made. Present your information to others in a small group. Invite your listeners to ask questions about your analysis.

Writing

▶ **A Free Writing** Write about one or more of the following topics.

- How do you feel about your handwriting? What does it show about your personality?
- How did you develop your handwriting? How has it changed?
- How would you compare your handwriting in your first and second languages?

▶ **B Topic Writing** Write about three or four of the important ideas you learned in the two chapter readings. Explain each idea as completely as possible. Refer to Chapter 1, pages 12 and 13, for guidelines to follow.

Read On: Taking It Further

Reading Journal

▶ **Retelling** There are some interesting stories about people who have overcome difficulty to achieve important goals in their lives. One example is the story of Harriet Tubman, a black woman who brought many people out of slavery in the 1860s. Another example is the story of Christopher Reeve, an actor who was paralyzed as the result of an accident but was determined to walk again. With your teacher's guidance, choose a story to read about and report on.

Newspaper Articles

▶ Check the newspaper or a news magazine over a few days and find an interesting article of courage and character like those you read in Chapter 13. Follow the steps for this activity on page 161 in Unit 4.

Word Play

Don't forget to write in your reading journal and add vocabulary log entries to your notebook. Show your entries to your teacher. Arrange to discuss your progress in reading. ■

▶ **A New-Fashioned Spelling Bee** Work in small groups of four or more. Form two teams within the group. Each team makes a list of ten to fifteen (or more!) important vocabulary words from any of the chapters in this unit. You can assign certain parts of the alphabet to avoid having words appear on both lists. Teams take turns asking the other team to spell a word on their list. The team to spell the most words correctly wins. You can make the game more difficult by varying the rules. Suggestions include using the word correctly in a sentence, spelling without writing, or spelling within a time limit.

 For additional activities, go to the *Reading Matters* Online Study Center at *college.hmco.com/pic/wholeytwo2e.*

UNIT 6

The Search for Answers

The fairest thing we can experience is the mysterious.

—*Albert Einstein*

Introducing the Topic

People are always interested in solving mysteries. Asking questions is an important key to solving mysteries. This unit is about topics that have fascinated and puzzled people for many years. In Chapter 16 you will share in the discovery of the world's oldest completely preserved man, the Iceman, and find out what can be learned from studying him. Chapter 17 examines what happened to the Titanic and what can be done to preserve this most famous of wrecks for the future. It also examines the interest in discovering wrecks under the sea. Chapter 18 is about the Anasazi. What led them to abandon their magnificent homes in the American Southwest?

Points of Interest

Finding Reasons

▷ **A** Write down your thoughts about this question on a separate piece of paper. Include three or more reasons.

What can we learn from studying the past and why is it important?

▷ **B** **Group Work** With your group, find the similarities and differences among your ideas. Make a list of three reasons for studying the past that your group can agree on. Present your list to your classmates.

Discussion Questions

▷ Think about these questions. Share your ideas with a partner or a small group.

1. What mysterious events have occurred in your lifetime?
2. If you had to solve a mystery, how would you do it?
3. What kinds of mysteries would these people solve: doctors, archaeologists, engineers, reporters, police officers? How would they do it?
4. Do you know of any important mysteries people are trying to solve today? Explain.

16 The Mystery of the Iceman

Chapter Openers

Discussion Questions

▶ Think about these questions. Share your ideas with a partner or a small group.

1. What is archaeology?
2. What famous archaeological sites do you know about? Where are they located?
3. Is it important to find out about the lives of prehistoric people? Why? What can we learn from studying them?
4. Can people visit prehistoric sites without destroying them?

Exploring and Understanding Reading

Predicting

▶ This reading is about the discovery of a 5,000-year-old man. What important information about this discovery do you think you might learn from this reading? List your ideas.

1. where the body was discovered
2. _____
3. _____
4. _____
5. _____

▶ Share your ideas with a partner or a small group.

Skimming

▶ **A** Read the complete story quickly and add to or change your prediction statements.

▶ **B** Reread the story and answer the following question.

Why was this discovery important?

_____

The Iceman of the Alps

1   On September 19, 1991, Helmut Simon and his wife, Erika, were on a hiking vacation in the Alps between Austria and Italy. They were walking alone, enjoying the views, when they noticed something sticking out of the snow. When they got close, they could see that it was a human head. Helmut noticed what looked like a hole in the back of the head. They wondered if this person could have been murdered. They decided to try to reach a phone and contact the police. The couple stopped at a hiker's shelter and told the owner about their discovery. The owner contacted both the Italian and Austrian police. The Italian police were too busy to investigate right away. The Austrian police were not able to come right away either.

2   The news of the discovery spread and over the next few days people did come. An Austrian police officer arrived first. He tried to take the body out of the ice with a jackhammer. This powerful machine ripped through the thick ice, but it also damaged part of the body. Fortunately, the jackhammer ran out of power before too much damage was done. Other people who heard about the discovery came and tried unsuccessfully to free the body. Finally, on September 23, Dr. Rainer Henn, a scientist who examines dead bodies, came to investigate. He immediately noticed that the body did not look white and waxy like most bodies do. It looked yellow and dry, like the body of a mummy. He borrowed a pickax and a ski pole and dug the body out.

3   Dr. Henn suspected that the body was very old. He transported the body by helicopter to Innsbruck, Austria. He wanted to get the body to a laboratory for tests to find out the man's age. In Innsbruck, the body was put in a coffin and kept in a warm room. Photographers and reporters were called in for a press conference. The room got warmer under the camera lights. People were smoking and touching the body. After a few hours, a fungus started growing on the body. Finally, Dr. Konrad Spindler, an archaeologist specializing in prehistoric man, was brought in. He was amazed by what he saw. He knew immediately that this was the body of a very ancient man; a man perhaps as much as 4,000 years old. And he also knew that the body would have to be moved to a refrigerated room to prevent further damage. The fungus was growing and the body was in danger. Dr. Spindler put the body into a cold, damp room with ninety-eight percent humidity at minus six degrees Celsius. Here the body was safe for scientists to study.

❹   Archaeologists from around the world wanted to study this Stone Age man. They made a number of exciting discoveries about the Iceman. First, tests showed that the Iceman was between 5,000 and 5,500 years old, making him the oldest completely preserved human being ever found. As they examined the body, archaeologists found some new things that tell us about very old human customs and behaviors. One of the discoveries was that there were strange markings, like tattoos, drawn on the man's back. Someone had made these tattoos. Before the Iceman, no one knew that tattooing was practiced that early. What was the significance of the tattoos? Were they religious symbols or the mark of a brave leader or hunter? The second interesting discovery was that his clothes were made of leather from the skins of three different animals. He had a cape made from grass. Who could have sewed his clothes? It looked as if someone skilled in sewing had made them. The Iceman's hair was only nine centimeters long and it was evenly cut. No one ever thought that people had been cutting their hair that long ago. Some mushrooms were found with the body. Were they used for medicine? The Iceman gave archaeologists a much more complete picture of the daily life of ancient people who lived fifty-three centuries ago.

❺   One of the questions that scientists had to consider was how the Iceman died. There were numerous theories. Some said that the Iceman fell to his death. Others disagreed. One of the most likely was that the Iceman had gotten caught in a sudden snowstorm and froze to death. The body had then dried out in the cold and had been covered over by ice. This would explain how the body came to be so well preserved. However, this theory was challenged when pathologists undertook extensive imaging of the body. Using an advanced type of X-ray called computerized tomography to produce a multi-dimensional image, they found an arrowhead lodged deep in the Iceman's left shoulder. The arrow would have torn through major blood vessels and broken the shoulder blade. It would seem as though he had been attacked. It is possible that he ran to escape his attackers and then collapsed due to his injuries. He probably lived only a few hours after he was attacked.

❻   The Iceman, who was named Oetzi, is now housed in a refrigerated cell at the archaeology museum in Bolzano, Italy, having been returned there after being kept for many years at the University of Innsbruck in Austria. Scientists want to continue studying the Iceman. Some would like to take tiny samples from the body for DNA analysis. This analysis would tell us about the man's genetic makeup and answer some important questions. What diseases had he had? How have human genes changed over the centuries? We could even discover who his closest living relatives are. The museum in Bolzano was built to preserve the Iceman and the tools and weapons that were found with him. Scientists feel strongly that the Iceman should be preserved for science and for future generations to study.

Chronology

▶ **Following the Story** Read the following statements. Number them according to their order in the story.

_____ a. The body is brought to Innsbruck.

_____ b. An Austrian police officer tries to remove the body with a jackhammer.

_____ c. Scientists discover the true age of the body.

_____ d. The Iceman and his possessions are studied by archaeologists.

_____ e. Scientists theorize about how the Iceman died.

_____ f. Helmut and Erika Simon see a body in the ice.

_____ g. The body is moved to a refrigerated room to prevent damage.

_____ h. The police are too busy to investigate.

_____ i. The body is housed in a museum in Bolzano, Italy.

_____ j. Dr. Konrad Spindler identifies the body as that of a prehistoric man.

_____ k. Dr. Henn examines the body.

_____ l. Scientists would like to study the body's DNA structure.

▶ Work with a partner to compare the order of the sentences. Together, locate and underline the information in the reading that matches the statements. Take turns reading the sentences aloud in the correct order.

Understanding Descriptive Details

▶ **A Connecting Words to Pictures** Look carefully at the sentences in the reading that describe what archaeologists found when they examined the Iceman. Use your scanning and guessing strategies to identify what is in these illustrations.

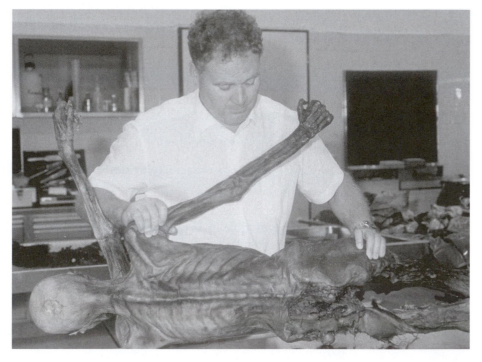

▶ **B Identifying Elements of a Story** An important part of this story is the work of different people to solve the mystery. Match the person or people in Column A to the work they did in Column B.

Column A

_____ 1. Helmut and Erika Simon

_____ 2. Italian police

_____ 3. An Austrian police officer

_____ 4. Dr. Rainer Henn

_____ 5. Dr. Konrad Spindler

_____ 6. Archaeologists

_____ 7. DNA scientists

_____ 8. Italians

Column B

a. want to find out what diseases he had and how he died.

b. made discoveries about the Iceman's daily life.

c. knew that the body was very old.

d. found the Iceman's body.

e. knew the body did not look like most dead bodies.

f. were too busy to investigate the body.

g. built a museum to house the Iceman.

h. tried to remove the body with a jackhammer.

▶ Work with a partner and take turns reading your sentences. Try to agree on the same answers. Look back at the reading if you disagree.

▶ **C Question Making** Scan the reading and find five questions that archaeologists and others asked about the Iceman. Underline the questions. Compare the questions you underlined with a partner.

Debating the Issues Today

▶ **Cloning** We have a rare opportunity to see and study the DNA of a person who lived 5,000 years ago. Scientists have already made remarkable discoveries based on their research studying the body. Should scientists be allowed to take cells from the Iceman to clone an individual using the DNA?

Prepare to debate this question by following these steps:

▶ **1.** Choose the side you will argue (clone an individual using cells from the Iceman's body or not).

2. Make a list of ideas in support of your position.

3. Work with one or more partners arguing the same position and add to your list of ideas.

4. Practice your oral presentation.

5. Present and argue your position against a person who prepared the other side.

6. Make a list of all the arguments for and against with your classmates. As a class, decide what you think should be done.

▶Vocabulary Building

Word Form and Meaning

▶ **A** Match the words in Column A with their meanings in Column B.

Column A	Column B
_____ 1. collapse	a. to carry or move something
_____ 2. confer	b. to find or uncover something
_____ 3. discover	c. to give to or discuss with others
_____ 4. signify	d. to fall down suddenly or break down in health
_____ 5. transport	e. to indicate or mean something

▶ **B** Study these five words and their forms: verb, noun, adjective, and adverb. Then choose the correct form for each part of speech in the chart on the next page. These words are commonly found in general and academic texts.

collapse (v.)	confer (v.)	discover (v.)	signify (v.)	transport (v.)
collapse (n.)	conference	discovery	signification	transportation
collapsing (adj.)	conferrable	discoverer	significance	transportable
collapsed (adj.)	conferring	discovered	significant	transporter
collapsible (adj.)		discoverable	significantly	transportability
			signified	transport
				transported

Verb	Noun	Adjective	Adverb
confer	1.	1.	
		2.	
discover	1.	1.	
	2.	2.	
signify	1.	1.	1.
	2.	2.	
transport	1.	1.	
	2.	2.	
	3.		
	4.		

► Compare lists with a partner. Try to agree on the same answers.

► **C** Write three or more sentences using words from the list.

► **D** In English we often add the suffix -er or -ist to the end of a root word to show what a person does. For example, a *teacher* is "a person who teaches," and an *artist* is "a person who creates works of art."

► Reread the text and find some examples of words that describe what people do and that end in -er, -ist, or -ian. Write the word and a definition in your own words.

Word   **Definition**

_____   _____

_____   _____

_____   _____

_____   _____

_____   _____

Vocabulary in Context

▶ **A** Use your understanding of one part of the sentence to help you guess the word that is missing. Your knowledge of English grammar will help you make the right choice.

Complete each sentence with one of the following verbs.

a. borrowed   b. contacted   c. grow   d. enjoy   e. investigated
f. move   g. noticed   h. prevent   i. suspected   j. touched

1. She _____ when she saw something that looked strange.

2. At first no one _____ that the body was that old.

3. He _____ the police and told them what happened.

4. The body was damaged because so many people had _____ it.

5. He _____ a pickax because he didn't have any tools of his own.

6. They _____ the tattoos on his back after they took off his clothes.

7. Some people want to _____ the body, but others want it to stay where it is.

8. She put on a bandage to _____ the cut from getting infected.

9. They wanted to visit the area and just _____ a walk in the mountains.

10. We didn't know that the fungus could _____ and spread so quickly.

▶ Check your answers. Work with a partner and take turns reading your sentences.

▶ **B Jigsaw Sentences** Use your understanding of key words to match each of the sentences in Column A with the sentence in Column B that would best follow it.

Column A

_____ 1. Some mushrooms were found with the body.

_____ 2. He had a cape made from grass.

_____ 3. He carried material for making a fire.

_____ 4. The body had strange markings on its back.

Column B

a. This was the first evidence that tattooing was practiced that long ago.

b. Were they used for medicine?

c. He kept this material in his backpack.

d. The clothes showed that someone skilled in sewing had made the garment.

▶ Work with a partner and take turns reading the sentence pairs.

Expanding Your Language

Reading

▶ Before reading the selection, read the following questions. After reading, answer them based on the information in the text.

1. What kind of food did the Iceman eat before he died?
2. What could have been the reason for the Iceman's death?
3. Where was the Iceman's body found?
4. What is the significance of the Iceman's last meal?
5. How did the scientists come to their conclusions?

Mummified Hunter Ate Well

A team of Italian scientists report that the Iceman had last meals that included venison and wild goat. The researchers also join their colleagues in imagining how he might have died. They suggest he might have been killed in a dispute among hunters. According to Franco Rollo of the University of Camerino, "Our investigation of his remains shows evidence that the Iceman was a high-ranked hunter." Although the Iceman's stomach was empty at the time of his death, the scientists were able to analyze the contents of his intestines. The Iceman's body was found frozen in a mountainous area, and pollen on his body indicated that he passed through a pine forest. On the way, he ate meat from an ibex, a type of wild goat once common in the Alps. He also ate cereal grains and some type of plant. Then, he ate another meal of red deer and, possibly, more grains. The findings add to the knowledge about Oetzi and the community he lived in. It shows that it was a mixed economy that included both hunting and farming. Because people living at this time usually ate small animals such as rabbit and squirrel, the fact that the Iceman ate only large animals adds to the idea that he was a person who was in a high social position in his community. The scientists made their conclusions based on comparing the DNA from the contents of his intestines with DNA from various animals and plants.

Speaking

▶ **Two-Minute Taped Talk** What did you learn about the discovery of the Iceman? Based on your own ideas and the information in this chapter, prepare a two-minute tape or CD to talk about the topic. Prepare your ideas before you record. Make a short outline of your ideas in note form. Practice your talk a few times before you record it. Give it to your teacher for feedback on content and clarity of ideas.

Writing

▶ **Topic Writing** Write about the topic of your taped talk. Follow the instructions in Chapter 1, pages 12 and 13.

 *Online Study Center*   For additional activities, go to the *Reading Matters* Online Study Center at *college.hmco.com/pic/wholeytwo2e*.

What Will Happen to the Titanic?

▶ Chapter Openers

Discussion Questions

▷ Think about these questions. Share your ideas with a partner or a small group.

1. What do you know about the story of the Titanic?
2. Why are people interested in the story of the Titanic?
3. What questions have people asked about the Titanic over the years?

▶ Paired Readings

▷ In this section, you will find two different stories on the same theme. Prepare to explain the story to someone who read the same story and then to a person who read the other story.

❶ The Tragedy of the Titanic

Skimming

▷ Read quickly and then answer the following questions.

1. Why was this ship so special?

_____

2. What was its fate?

_____

▷ Work with a partner to compare your answers.

Titanic Lost!

By Robert D. Ballard

It's Wednesday, April 10, 1912, and hundreds of people are arriving in Southampton, England, for the adventure of a lifetime—the maiden voyage of the R.M.S. Titanic.

The ship is unsinkable, a marvel of modern engineering. She's an enormous structure—882 feet long, weighs 42,000 tons, and, if stood on end, would rise higher than the pyramids of Egypt and tower over the Washington monument.

She's a floating palace. A first-class one-way ticket would cost up to $50,000 today.

So Much to See, So Little Time

Excitement fills the air as the children explore this great ship that will carry them across the Atlantic Ocean. So many things to see and all of them brand new.

The carpets are thick, the linens clean, and the big dining rooms lined with rich wooden paneling. There are even elevators to carry people from deck to deck, down into the bowels of the ship—where the swimming pool and squash court are found.

It's hard to sleep the first night for fear of missing something wonderful. But fatigue overtakes the travelers as the sounds of the band drift off into the dark chilly night.

Each day brings new adventure, but just as it begins to seem the cruise could never end, word comes that the ship is approaching the shore of Canada. New York City is not so far away.

Quick Conferences in the Radio Room

That night, April 14, the older children are allowed to stay up a little longer. Some peek into the windows of the radio operators. There they see the radioman, Jack Phillips, but he is too busy to notice.

Just then another man walks into the radio room. It's hard to hear him talk—but it's something about icebergs. Phillips hands a note to his assistant, Harold Bride, who quickly disappears.

The children want to explore the bridge, but it's getting cold. Time to head off to a warm, soft bed.

Iceberg, Dead Ahead!

Huddled in the crow's nest high on the forward main mast is the lookout, Fred Fleet. As he stares out into the dark eternal night, he suddenly sees something straight ahead.

"Iceberg: right ahead!" he yells.

He quickly calls the bridge, but there is not much they can do. The ship is traveling too fast. As she turns to port (left) the iceberg passes down the starboard (right) side. Fleet braces for the collision.

But surprisingly it doesn't seem too bad, just a gentle nudge as a few chunks of ice fall onto the deck. The iceberg disappears in the ship's wake as some of the passengers playfully throw bits of the iceberg at each other.

The Ship Is Going to Sink in One Hour

Below decks, it's a different situation. There Captain Edward J. Smith and the Titanic's builder, Thomas Andrews, find water pouring into the mail room, the forward holds, and the two boiler rooms.

The hole in the side of the ship doesn't seem to be large. But it's not the size of the hole that seems to be bothering Andrews—it's the length of the damage. The Titanic can float if four of her sixteen watertight compartments are flooded. But water is flowing into at least five.

Quickly Andrews completes his mental calculations and turns to Captain Smith. "The ship is gong to sink in an hour to an hour and a half," he reports grimly.

The captain is stunned. He knows that there aren't enough lifeboats for everyone aboard. The ship's owners hadn't thought them necessary.

A Desperate Call for Help

Returning to the bridge, Captain Smith tells the radio operator to send out a series of distress calls. Perhaps there is help nearby. On the horizon to the north he can see the lights of a ship. Maybe the radio operator can raise the crew. Maybe they will see the distress rockets. He orders them shot into the still night.

Initially, the lateness of the night, the calmness of the sea, and the ship's soft impact with the iceberg lull the passengers into thinking that nothing is really wrong. They are on the Titanic, aren't they? Isn't she unsinkable?

At first the passengers don't want to climb into the lifeboats. They can't even see the surface of the sea far below. Why would anyone want to leave this wonderful ship and venture into a cold, dark world in a tiny boat? It seems so nice on the boat deck where the band is now playing. But the boats are lowered anyway. Many are half empty as they row away toward the light on the distant northern horizon.

Now Only Death Awaits

It is only when the Titanic begins to take on a severe downward angle that the passengers begin to realize that only death awaits them.

Panic breaks out as everyone rushes to the stern only to find that there are no more lifeboats left. In desperation they begin jumping into the sea—a sea so cold that they are dead within an hour. The sounds of their screams are mixed with the even louder death groans of the ship.

Then a chilling silence falls across the surface of the sea. What began as the greatest sea voyage of all time has ended in great disaster. Of the more than 2,200 people aboard moments ago, only 705 are saved. The Titanic is gone forever—or is she?

Scanning for Descriptive Details

 Reading Tip

Marking the **question number** in the **margin** of a **text** is another way to locate the information for your answers quickly. ■

Look back at the reading for the answers to these questions. Mark the question number in the margin of the page. Write your answers in note form.

1. What luxuries did the ship offer its passengers?

_____

2. What happened on the night of April 14, 1912?

_____

3. What message did the ship's builder give the captain?

_____

4. a. What was the captain's reaction?

   _____

   b. Why did he react this way?

   _____

   c. What did he give orders to do?

   _____

5. How did the passengers react to the accident at first?

_____

6. When did the passengers start to panic?

_____

7. How did the tragedy end?

_____

Work with a partner to ask and answer the questions. Compare the information you marked in the margin.

Note Taking

▶ **Chronology of Events** Scan the reading quickly and find ten to twelve facts about the events that took place aboard the Titanic the night of the sinking. Note these facts in the order they occurred.

Events on the Titanic the Night of April 14

1. radio operator receives message about icebergs / too busy to notice

2. _____

3. _____

4. _____

5. _____

6. _____

7. _____

8. _____

9. _____

10. _____

11. _____

12. _____

Recapping the Events

▶ Work with a partner who took notes about the same story. Take turns explaining several of the facts to each other. As you talk, be sure to explain the events in the order they occurred. Check to make sure that you both have the same information. Add or correct any facts you need to.

❷The Titanic Rediscovered

Skimming   ▶ Read the selection quickly and then answer the following questions.

1. Why was this search different from others?

_____

2. When did they find the Titanic?

_____

▶ Work with a partner to compare your answers.

Titanic Found!

By Robert D. Ballard

When the R.M.S. Titanic was lost in 12,500 feet of water in 1912, no one thought that she would ever be found. A series of attempts was made in the 1980s, but all failed to locate the shipwreck.

But during the summer of 1985, my team from the Woods Hole (Massachusetts) Oceanographic Institution found the Titanic sitting right-side up on the bottom of the Atlantic Ocean. The world was amazed to hear "The Titanic found!"

Why did our search prove successful when others failed?

The answer lay in our key strategy. When the Titanic struck an iceberg on April 14, 1912, it opened a wound in the starboard (right) side of the ship. Water rushed into the forward compartments, causing her to sink at the bow.

Slowly her giant stern began to rise into the air, creating stress on the weaker midsection of the ship. Ships of her design had large dining areas and salons in the central part of the ship, rooms that could not support the full weight of the stern. So as her stern rose even higher there

was a sudden, tremendous noise and rush of air as the ship split in half.

As the hull began to tear, all sorts of objects poured into the sea. Titanic's massive boilers, her safes, cooking pots, dishes, tons of coal, everything imaginable began a free fall to the bottom.

A Mile of Debris

As these objects fell, the ocean current that brought the icebergs from the north swept the objects away. The lighter the object, the farther it was swept. Some items fell through the surface currents in a few minutes. But many objects, like the deck furniture, lingered in the current longer. The lifeboats carrying the survivors drifted for hours.

By the time all the objects had finally come to rest on the bottom, they created a trail of debris more than one mile long.

We looked for the debris trail, not the ship. That's why we were so interested in the log book of the Californian—the ship the people on the Titanic had seen that night drifting on the northern horizon. The Californian shut down her engines that night to avoid the icebergs, but her logbook would show valuable information about the currents that caused the ship to drift to the south. Once we knew about these currents, we could set our search strategy.

Up and Back, Up and Back

We began in the area where the Carpathia, the first rescue ship to arrive, had picked up Titanic's lifeboats. We knew the Titanic's hull could *not* be south of this location.

Once there, we lowered our towed camera system, Argo, more than two miles to just above the bottom of the ocean and began a series of long search lines running east to west, perpendicular to the trail of debris we were looking for.

As we completed our westerly line, we turned north for one mile before turning back to the east to begin another long search line.

Slowly we progressed toward the Californian's position. Then, on September 1, 1985, Argo's sensitive cameras passed over the trail of debris we were looking for.

At first, we saw small, light objects, but as we continued, the objects that we saw were heavier and heavier, until suddenly one of the Titanic's massive boilers passed under Argo. Then we saw the ship's gigantic stern.

The Titanic was finally found!

Scanning for Descriptive Details

▶ Look back at the reading for the answers to these questions. Mark the question number in the margin of the page. Write your answers in note form.

1. How deep did the Titanic sink?

_____

2. Why did the bow sink and the stern rise?

_____

3. Why did the ship split in two?

_____

4. What happened to the contents of the ship after it split?

_____

5. How were the objects from the ship affected by the ocean currents?

_____

6. What did Ballard's team look for?

_____

7. Where did the team begin its search?

_____

8. How did the team carry out its search?

_____

▶ Work with a partner to ask and answer the questions. Look back at the reading and indicate where you marked the information.

Note Taking

▶ **Chronology of Events** Scan the reading and find ten to twelve facts about the events Ballard studied in the search for the Titanic. Write these facts in note form in the order they occurred.

The Search for the Wreck of the Titanic

1. April 14, 1912, hit iceberg / opened hole in right side / water rushed in at bow

2. _____

3. _____

4. _____

5. _____

6. _____

7. _____

8. _____

9. _____

10. _____

11. _____

12. _____

Recapping the Events

▶ Work with a partner who took notes about the same story. Take turns explaining several of the facts to each other. As you talk, be sure to explain the events in the order they occurred. Check to make sure that you both have the same information. Add or correct any facts you need to.

Comparing the Readings

Creating a Chronology

▶ Scan your notes and the reading for dates, times, and the sequence or order of the events in this story of the Titanic. Note this information in order in the following format.

Event: _____

Time: _____

Event: _____

Time: _____

▶ Work with a partner who prepared a different reading. Make an oral report of these events to your partner. As your partner speaks, note the events your partner reports on and include the events from both readings in your list.

Reacting to the Story

▶ Return to the discussion questions at the beginning of this chapter. Talk about these questions again. Add new ideas that you learned from the readings. Discuss these additional questions.

1. Do you think the accident could have been avoided? How?
2. Could more people have been saved?
3. What did people learn from this tragedy?

Giving Your Opinion

▶ Read the following selection and discuss these questions with a partner or with others in a small group.

1. Why are people so interested in the Titanic that they would spend large amounts of money to visit the site?
2. Should visitors to the Titanic be banned or not?

▶ Share your opinions with your classmates.

Trying to Save the Titanic

When Robert Ballard discovered the Titanic in 1985, he was amazed at how well preserved it was. It had separated into two pieces, its bow was a kilometer away from its stern, but the insides of the ship were still intact. Ballard and others returned to the site of the discovery several times to videotape the sunken ship. Many people wanted to see what the wreckage looked like. Some people wanted to bring parts of the ship up to the surface. Since its discovery, the place where the Titanic sank off the coast of Newfoundland has been a big attraction for divers, scientists, filmmakers, and tourists. Artificial flowers and about a dozen plaques have been left on the decks. But, according to Capt. Craig McLean, ocean exploration director at the National Oceanic and Atmospheric Administration, who led a dive in June 2003, some people have left garbage behind—even beer and soda bottles.

Now scientists and other experts say that the wreckage is almost completely covered with microbes called rusticles that are eating the ship. After seven decades under the salty water, the Titanic is decaying very fast. The thirty-meter forward mast has collapsed nearly a decade earlier than previously predicted. And the crow's nest from which a lookout shouted, "Iceberg, right ahead!" has disappeared. In 1996, scientists found that bacteria in the rusticles were consuming 90 kilograms of iron from the ship each day. Two years later, they returned to find that the microbes were removing 272 kilograms of iron a day. In 2001, the U.S. National Oceanic and Atmospheric Administration estimated that "the hull and structure of the ship may collapse to the ocean floor within the next fifty years, perhaps sooner."

For more than ninety years, the world's most famous sea wreck lay on the Atlantic floor, preserved in time. Now, it is beginning to rust away—and human activity may be the problem. According to Ed Kamuda, president of the Titanic Historical Society in Springfield, Massachusetts, human activity, including tourism and expeditions, needs to be limited. For $36,000, anyone can visit the site in a mini submarine, known as a submersible. "Every time they go down there, they do damage. The propellers stir up the rusticles," Kamuda said. "If they would just leave it alone, it would last a lot longer."

Vocabulary Building

Word Form and Meaning

▷ **A** Match the words in Column A with their meanings in Column B.

Column A

_____ 1. locate

_____ 2. predict

_____ 3. separate

_____ 4. strategize

_____ 5. structure

Column B

a. to tell that something will happen in advance

b. to build, organize, or arrange something

c. to find or look for someone or something

d. to keep apart or divide someone or something

e. to make one or more plans or designs

▶ **B** Study these five words and their forms: verb, noun, adjective, and adverb. Then choose the correct form for each part of speech in the chart below. These words are commonly found in general and academic texts.

locate (v.)	predict (v.)	separate (v.)	strategize (v.)	structure (v.)
location (n.)	predictor	separation	strategy	structure
locator (n.)	prediction	separable	strategic	structural
locatable (adj.)	predicted	separator	strategically	structurally
located (adj.)	predictable	separateness	strategizer	structured
	predictably	separate		
		separately		

Verb	Noun	Adjective	Adverb
predict	1. 2.	1. 2.	1.
separate	1. 2. 3.	1. 2.	1.
strategize	1. 2.	1.	1.
structure	1.	1. 2.	1.

▶ Compare lists with a partner. Try to agree on the same answers.

▶ **C** Write three or more sentences using words from the list.

▶ D Synonyms Match the words in Column A with the words in Column B that have a similar meaning.

Column A

_____ 1. discover

_____ 2. drift

_____ 3. lower

_____ 4. nudge

_____ 5. overtake

_____ 6. peek

_____ 7. search

_____ 8. stare

_____ 9. support

_____10. surface

_____11. tear

_____12. enormous

Column B

a. rise

b. bump

c. help

d. surpass

e. cut

f. find

g. move slowly

h. very large

i. move down

j. gaze

k. glance

l. hunt

▶ E Descriptive Language Adjectives are words that describe things. Scan the readings in this chapter and notice the different adjectives that are used. Try to find different types of adjectives: those ending in -er, like *bigger*; those ending in -est, like *biggest*; those ending in -ing, like *charming*; and simple adjectives like *gentle*.

Find a synonym or antonym for each word on your list. Work with a partner to compare your lists.

Vocabulary in Context

▶ **Using Context Clues** You can often understand the meaning of a new word from your understanding of the other words in a sentence.

▶ Complete each sentence with one of the following verbs.

| a. approached | b. carry | c. created | d. estimated | e. explore |
| f. raise | g. report | h. split | i. stared | j. traveled |

1. The sinking of the Titanic _____ panic when it was reported in the news.

2. The builders _____ that it would take about three to five days to sink the Titanic.

3. The ship was so big that it took days to _____ it all.

4. The expedition leaders had to _____ enough money to carry out their research.

5. The Titanic's stern rose out of the water and then the ship _____ into two pieces.

6. She knew that she had to _____ the accident she had seen.

7. He looked intently and _____ into the darkness trying to find the right road to take.

8. The ship was moving fast, and after a few days it _____ the coast of Canada.

9. It was the first time she had ever _____ to another part of the world.

10. There were elevators to _____ people to the different parts of the ship.

Expanding Your Language

Reading

▶ Before reading the selection, read the following questions. After reading, answer them based on the information in the text.

1. What is involved in finding a wreck at the bottom of the ocean today?
2. Who was Antoine de Saint-Exupéry? What mystery surrounds his death?
3. What discovery has now been made?
4. What aviation accomplishments did Saint-Exupéry achieve?
5. Why did the salvage operation take as long as it did?
6. What mystery still remains?

Locating the Little Prince

In today's world, the ocean is less able to keep its secrets. There are numerous salvage companies and individuals who are ready with the latest technology to locate wrecks at the bottom of the sea. But locating a wreck is only the first step in solving a mystery. The challenge is to carry out the salvage in a way that honors the memory of those who died. One of the mysteries of the Second World War was the disappearance of Antoine de Saint-Exupéry, the author of the world famous novel, *The Little Prince. The Little Prince* is a story of one person's search for the meaning of life that has been translated into more than 150 languages. Saint-Exupéry was flying a reconnaissance mission over France near the end of the Second World War. He never returned from the mission. Almost one year later, when it seemed clear that he had died, a funeral mass was held for him. But, the body of Saint-Exupéry was never recovered and the wreckage of his plane was never found.

Saint-Exupéry has long been considered a hero in France. He was an enthusiastic aviator and he loved to take chances in the air. He first learned to fly in 1921. In the 1920s, he spent three years flying over the Sahara desert in northern Africa to deliver the mail. During that time he learned to love the desert, flying over it in an open cockpit plane. He narrowly escaped death several times. In 1929, he moved to South America and established the Aeropostale's air delivery service there. He could not imagine himself anywhere but in the cockpit of an airplane. Some say he even wrote his books while flying. It was his life-long passion. Although he was too old for military service, he insisted on returning to fight for France during the Second World War. He rejoined the French Air Force in northern Africa. On July 31, 1944, he took off on his final mission.

In 1988, a fisherman off the coast of Marseilles discovered Saint-Exupéry's silver identification bracelet in his net. Now, six decades after he disappeared, a French underwater salvage team has discovered the remains of the plane he was flying when he disappeared. The salvage operation that identified the remains of Saint-Exupéry's plane said it was found in 230 feet of water off Marseilles in the same area where a fisherman had found the bracelet. Salvage operations were delayed two years until officials for the French Culture Ministry could approve the dive. The head of the Culture Ministry announced the discovery and said that it was now formally established that the author's plane had gone down off of Marseilles. But the reason it did is not known and probably never will be. This final part of his life still remains a mystery.

Speaking

▶ **Two-Minute Taped Talk** Choose a part of the Titanic story that interests you. It can be about the night the ship sank, the discovery of the ship at the bottom of the ocean, or how you feel about bringing up the Titanic from the sea. Based on your own ideas and the information in this chapter, prepare a two-minute audiotape or audio CD to talk about the Titanic. Make a short outline of your ideas in note form. Practice your talk a few times before you record it.

Writing

▶ **A** **Topic Writing** Use the chronology you created to write about what happened to the Titanic.

▶ **B** **Reaction Writing** Write about a part of the Titanic story that you find interesting, and tell why it interests you.

 *Online Study Center*   For additional activities, go to the *Reading Matters* Online Study Center at *college.hmco.com/pic/wholeytwo2e*.

18 The Anasazi: Why Did They Leave?

Chapter Openers

Chapter Openers

Using Illustrations to Understand Ideas

▶ Look at the different activities in the illustrations on the next page. Then read each of the following sentences and write the letter of the illustration that matches each sentence.

1. _____ There are beautiful drawings on the walls of the cliff dwellings.

2. _____ The Anasazi built round kivas for religious worship.

3. _____ They made beautiful baskets and pottery.

4. _____ People had to climb up and down steep rocks to reach food and water on the mesa.

5. _____ It was a center of trade and agriculture for the native peoples.

6. _____ The cliff dwellings could be very cold and damp in the winter.

7. _____ The rooms were smoky from the fires needed for warmth and cooking.

8. _____ The Anasazi grew corn, beans, and squash for food.

▶ Work with a partner. Take turns reading each of the statements. Agree on the matches you chose. Then discuss this question:

What do you think were the joys and difficulties of the life shown in these pictures?

A.

B.

C.

D.

Exploring and Understanding Reading

Predicting

▶ This reading is about the mystery of why the Anasazi made and abandoned their homes. What do you think you might find out from this reading? List your ideas in note form.

1. How the cliff dwellings were discovered

2. _____

3. _____

4. _____

5. _____

▶ Share your ideas with a partner or a small group.

Skimming

▶ Read all the paragraphs quickly. Add to or change your prediction statements.

Scanning for Facts

▶ Read the questions after each paragraph. Find the answers in the reading. Underline the key words and write the answers in note form.

Mystery of the Southwest

❶   Mesa Verde is a flat-topped plateau located in the southwest part of the United States. In this part of the country, the climate is generally dry. The mesa rises up to a height of 8,572 feet (2,613 meters). In Spanish, Mesa Verde means "green table." The top of the mesa is covered with green plants and trees. Throughout Mesa Verde there are steep canyons. There is little water at the top of the mesa and even less in the canyons. Water comes from the winter snowfall and spring and summer rains. In the summer, temperatures can reach into the 90s (Fahrenheit), but in the winter, they can drop to 0 degrees. Today, this area is part of Mesa Verde National Park. The park preserves and protects the culture of the Anasazi people. The beauty and mystery of this place reflect the spirit of those ancient people who once lived here. The park is a World Heritage cultural site and each year is visited by more than 800,000 people from all over the world.

1. Where is Mesa Verde located?

_____

2. Why is Mesa Verde called "green table"?

_____

3. What is the climate of the area like?

_____

4. Where does the water come from?

_____

5. What is the purpose of Mesa Verde National Park?

_____

6. Who visits this area today?

_____

---

❷   Mesa Verde was the center of life for the Anasazi who lived in the area hundreds of years ago, between the sixth and the fourteenth centuries (A.D. 500–1300). It was a center for trade and agriculture for the native peoples who lived in the Four Corners area of what are today the states of Utah, Colorado, New Mexico, and Arizona. We know very little about the area's history from the 1400s to the late 1800s. In the early 1870s, American settlers first began to visit and document their exploration of this area. By the late 1800s, ranchers herding their cattle began to wander into the canyons. Here they discovered the ruins of a great lost civilization. They came across magnificent houses made out of stone in the sides of the canyon cliffs. Inside they found pottery, baskets, wall art, and tools made from stone. The ranchers were amazed and overwhelmed by the beauty of what they had found. They asked themselves many questions. Who had lived there, and why had these people built homes in the steep canyons? How did they survive? Finally, they wondered why the people had abandoned their cliff dwellings.

---

1. When did the Anasazi live at Mesa Verde?

_____

2. Where was the trade center of native peoples?

_____

3. When did Americans first explore the area?

_____

4. What did the ranchers find in the canyons?

_____

5. a. How did ranchers react to seeing the cliff dwellings?

_____

   b. What questions did they ask themselves?

_____

---

❸   Soon after the discovery of Mesa Verde, archaeologists came to study the cliff dwellings. They found evidence of hundreds of houses built into the sides of the cliffs during the years A.D. 1100 to 1300. The Anasazi had carved out the sandstone rock with simple tools made from stone and wood. Archaeologists have found about six hundred dwellings in the canyons. Some accommodations, such as Cliff Palace, are very large, but most of the dwellings are smaller in size. There are beautiful drawings on the walls of the cliff dwellings. It appears that the Anasazi would begin their dwellings by constructing round kivas. The kivas are small rooms cut into the ground that people entered from above. They were used for religious worship. The number of these structures show the important role that religion played in Anasazi life. Every building had a kiva. In Cliff Palace there are twenty-three kivas.

---

1. How many dwellings have been found in the canyons at Mesa Verde?

_____

2. When were the houses built?

_____

3. a. How were the kivas constructed?

_____

   b. What was their purpose?

_____

4. How do we know the kivas were important?

_____

> ❹   Archaeologists have some ideas about the Anasazi's daily life at Mesa Verde. The early Anasazi were hunter-gatherers. They used wood and stone to make tools—bows and arrows and simple knives for hunting. They ate a simple diet. In the later periods of their civilization, the Anasazi learned to grow corn, beans, and squash. These crops grew well during the long 161–172-day growing season. These foods were a healthy addition to their traditional diet of meat from the deer and bighorn sheep they hunted, and the berries and other plants they gathered. The Anasazi made useful items, such as beautiful baskets and pottery covered with distinctive black geometric designs that they used to carry and cook food and water. In the early periods, the Anasazi lived on the top of the mesas. Then, for some unknown reason, they moved into the canyons. They built new homes in the sides of the cliffs. Life in the cliff dwellings was difficult. The rooms were cold and damp in the winter and smoky from the fires needed for warmth and cooking. It was hard to get in and out of their homes. Using only their hands and feet, the Anasazi had to climb up and down the steep rocks to reach food and water on the mesa. This climbing would have been difficult for older people and very dangerous for young children who could fall easily. Most of the Anasazi were under five feet tall and generally lived only into their twenties or thirties. The bodies found in the area show that people suffered from medical problems such as arthritis, tooth decay, broken bones, and lung disease.

1. What kinds of tools did the Anasazi use?

_____

2. a. What items did they make for the home?

_____

   b. What did they use these items for?

_____

3. What was their diet?

_____

4. Why did they move from the mesa to the canyons?

_____

5. What two things were difficult about living in the cliff dwellings?

   a. _____

   b. _____

6. What medical facts show us that the Anasazi had difficult lives?

_____

---

5   By the end of the Great Pueblo period, the Anasazi had moved from smaller cliff dwellings into larger dwellings that could hold a number of families. These larger dwellings were better built and could be defended more easily. Mutual support, increased productivity, and innovation in technology resulted from life in these communal dwellings. The construction of interconnected and large-scale kivas shows an increased emphasis on religion in the Anasazi society. Religious ceremonies might have helped build a spirit of unity among the people. But this great civilization came to an abrupt end sometime between the years 1200 and 1300. The Anasazi abandoned their cliff houses and never returned. What happened to make the Anasazi leave their homes forever is still a mystery today. There are different theories but no certain answers.

---

1. Why did the Anasazi move into larger dwellings?

_____

2. When did the Anasazi leave Mesa Verde?

_____

3. What mystery still remains?

_____

▶ Work with a partner to ask and answer the questions. Look back at the reading if you cannot agree on the answers.

Finding the Main Ideas

▶ Quickly read the beginning and ending of each paragraph. Write the main idea of each paragraph in note form. The main idea of Paragraph 1 is given as an example.

Main Ideas: Mystery of the Southwest

Paragraph 1:   *Description of Mesa Verde*

Paragraph 2:   _____

Paragraph 3:   _____

Paragraph 4:   _____

Paragraph 5:   _____

▶ Work with a partner to compare and refine your ideas. Try to agree on the same ideas. Check your ideas with your teacher.

Applying the Information

▶ **A Theorizing** Based on the information in the first reading, what could be some reasons that the Anasazi abandoned their homes and never returned? With a partner or a small group, make a list of theories and choose two or three reasons you can agree on. Share your ideas with your classmates.

▶ **B** Read the following paragraphs and highlight the different theories about the Anasazi's departure.

The Mystery of the Cliff Dwellers

There are many theories to explain why the Anasazi abandoned their cliff dwellings and left the area. One theory is that they left because a drought occurred and there wasn't enough water to survive. Because the main sources of water were snow and rain, a long period of dry weather could have reduced the water supply. There is evidence that it was extremely dry and cold at this time. Cold weather would have affected the production of corn, the main food source for the Anasazi. Without corn, a famine could have begun. Also their farming methods might have caused more food problems. Burning the land and removing all the trees damaged the soil, so less food would grow. Without trees, animals may have moved out of the hunting grounds within reach of the Anasazi. Linked to the problem of food supply is the problem of overpopulation. During this period the population had grown, reaching about five thousand. With so many people there probably wasn't a large enough supply of wood to build and make fires.

One controversial theory is that the Anasazi moved into cliff houses to better defend themselves against enemies. There is disagreement over this theory. Those who disagree say there are no physical signs of violence in the area. But those who favor the theory argue that the strong walls and high cliffs brought the Anasazi into the canyons. Any attackers would have had to climb up and down steep rocks to fight. In times of famine (when there is no food) and drought (when there is no water), it is easy to imagine that fighting would start. If this fighting grew too intense or too difficult, then the Anasazi might have decided to abandon the canyons. Added to all this is evidence that the Anasazi could use fires as a system of signaling from different points in the canyons. Perhaps, then, it was possible for groups to communicate with one another.

A final theory is that the religious leaders might have convinced the people to move. The increase in the size and amount of kiva construction shows evidence of the greater importance of religion in Anasazi life. Perhaps the priests, who traveled the most between the different groups, convinced the Anasazi that their gods would lead them to a new and better place.

Using Highlighting to Make a List

▶ From the information that you highlighted, list the theories about why the Anasazi abandoned their cliff dwellings.

1. _____

2. _____

3. _____

4. _____

5. _____

Giving Your Opinion

▶ What theories explaining why the Anasazi left their cliff dwellings do you think are the most believable? Number the theories from most believable (1) to least believable (5). Discuss your list with a partner or a small group. Try to agree on the order in your group. Report your opinions to your classmates.

Debating the Issues Today

Recently, park officials in the Southwest have become worried that the large number of tourists will damage the environment and destroy important evidence of ancient life in the area. For example, bringing cars and other vehicles over dirt roads has caused roads in some places to weaken and wash away in the spring. Using jeeps and other off-road vehicles, people can reach places that were previously undisturbed. Archaeologists are afraid that the tourists will disturb important sites before they can be examined. The danger of fires in these dry areas is also a concern. Some officials think that these areas should be closed or restricted to tourists. Others feel that people should be encouraged to visit national parks for both educational and economic reasons. What is your opinion?

Consider the following idea:

More people should be encouraged to visit National Parks.

Prepare to debate the idea by following the steps in Chapter 16, page 214.

Vocabulary Building

Word Form and Meaning

A Match the words in Column A with their meanings in Column B.

Column A

_____ 1. abandon

_____ 2. accommodate

_____ 3. innovate

_____ 4. preserve

_____ 5. protect

Column B

a. to keep someone or something from changing or being damaged

b. to invent or make something new

c. to help someone or make room for someone or something

d. to guard or keep from danger

e. to leave behind or give up

B Study these five words and their forms: verb, noun, adjective, and adverb. Then choose the correct form for each part of speech in the chart on the next page. These words are commonly found in general and academic texts.

abandon (v.)	accommodate (v.)	innovate (v.)	preserve (v.)	protect (v.)
abandonment (n.)	accommodative	innovation	preservative	protector
abandoned (adj.)	accommodating	innovatively	preservation	protection
	accommodatingly	innovator	preserved	protected
	accommodation	innovative	preserving	protective
		innovated	preserver	protectively
				protecting

Verb	Noun	Adjective	Adverb
accommodate	1.	1.	1.
		2.	
innovate	1.	1.	1.
	2.	2.	
preserve	1.	1.	
	2.	2.	
	3.		
protect	1.	1.	1.
	2.	2.	
		3.	

▶ Compare lists with a partner. Try to agree on the same answers.

▶ **C** Write three or more sentences using words from the list.

▶ **D** Read each sentence and circle the correct word to use in the sentence. Write *N* if the word is a noun or *V* if the word is a verb.

1. _____ The people loved the **draw** / **drawings** that the Anasazi carved into the rock.

2. _____ We don't know why people decided to move into the cliff **dwell** / **dwellings**.

3. _____ People needed to be strong because **climb** / **climbing** the rocks wasn't easy.

4. _____ The **survive** / **survival** of the Anasazi depended on having enough food and water for the winter months.

5. _____ Perhaps it was a **combine** / **combination** of drought and cold weather that forced the people to move.

6. _____ They needed the cliff dwellings to **protect** / **protection** themselves from the cold.

7. _____ The park receives over 800,000 **visit** / **visitors** each year.

8. _____   We don't know why the Anasazi decided to
abandon / **abandonment** their cliff dwellings.

9. _____   The Anasazi were able to **produce** / **production** beautiful baskets
and pottery for use in cooking and carrying water and food.

10. _____   There was a **reduce** / **reduction** in the number of animals the
Anasazi could find to hunt.

Vocabulary in Context

▶ **A Jigsaw Sentences** Use your understanding of key words to match each of the
sentence beginnings in Column A with the ending in Column B that fits best.

Column A

_____ 1. The Anasazi
civilization

_____ 2. Climbing out of the
canyons

_____ 3. The top of the mesa

_____ 4. The park

_____ 5. Cliff Palace

_____ 6. The kiva

Column B

a. is used for religious purposes.

b. is carved out of the sandstone rock.

c. is covered with green plants.

d. existed between the sixth and
fourteenth centuries.

e. is difficult for old people and children.

f. is visited by people from all over the
world.

▶ Check your answers with a partner, then take turns reading your answers.

▶ **B Possibility** The words *might, could,* and *would* are verbs or modal forms that
show possibility. Many of the theories about the Anasazi are presented as possibilities.
Scan the readings and find two sentences with each of these verb or modal forms.
Highlight or underline the sentences. Write two sentences of your own using these
forms.

might

1. _____

2. _____

could

1. _____

2. _____

would

1. _____

2. _____

Expanding Your Language

Speaking

▶ **Role Play/Interviewing** Use the notes you made about Mesa Verde and the life of the Anasazi to role-play an interview between a reporter and an archaeologist. Prepare five or six questions for your partner. Take turns asking these questions and giving answers.

Writing

▶ **Descriptions** Write about a historical place you know of and what goes on there. Describe the place and the activity in as much detail as possible.

Read On: Taking It Further

Reading Suggestions

▶ Find some readings or topics like the ones in this unit that you are interested in at your reading level. For example, you could find an easy-reading edition of *The Iceman* by Don Lessem, or of *The Titanic* by Robert Ballard. A good source of reading material is your bookstore or library's magazine and newspaper section.

Other Suggestions

View your **reading journal** and **vocabulary log** entries. Review your use of reading skills and strategies. Write a response to the following question: How has your reading improved? ▪

▶ Television programs have been made about the Titanic, the Iceman, and the Anasazi. Movies have been made about the Titanic. Try to find out if one of these programs or movies is available through your library or video store. Ask your teacher for help in locating these programs and watching them. Talk about what you watched with your classmates.

 For additional activities, go to the *Reading Matters* Online Study Center at *college.hmco.com/pic/wholeytwo2e.*

◗Text Credits

p. 28: Graphic from "How Drowsiness Shapes the Day," David F. Dinges, Roger J. Broughton (editors), *Sleep and Alertness: Chronobiological, Behavioral, and Medical Aspects of Napping*. Copyright © 1989 Raven Press. Reprinted with permission of David F. Dinges.

pp. 121–122: "Saving the Sky," from J. Kelly Beatty, "Licking Light Pollution," *Night Sky*, September/October 2004, Vol. 1, Issue 3. Copyright © Sky Publishing Corp. Reprinted with permission.

pp. 127–128: "The Joys of Stargazing," based on the story, "The Father of Street-Corner Stargazing," by Brett Campbell, *The Wall Street Journal*, September 1, 2004. Used with permission of the author.

pp. 148–150: "Global Water Shortages," extracts from "Global Water Shortages" by Mary H. Cooper, *CQ Researcher*, December 15, 1995, Vol. 5, No. 47, pp. 1113-1136. Copyright © 1995 by Congressional Quarterly, Inc. Used with permission.

pp. 159–160: "Coming Together to Save a River," by Martin Rosenberg, *The New York Times*, March 16, 2004. Copyright © 2004 by The New York Times Co. Reprinted with permission.

pp. 167–168: "With a Little Help from Her Friends," from *Newsweek*, 5/29/1995 © 1995 Newsweek, Inc. All rights reserved. Reprinted by permission.

pp. 200–201: "The Lowdown on Handwriting Analysis," extract from "The Lowdown on Handwriting Analysis," by M. Scanlon and J. Mauro, *Psychology Today*, November/December 1992. Reprinted with permission from Psychology Today Magazine. Copyright © 1992 Sussex Publishers, Inc.